EMCDDA SCIENTIFIC MONOGRAPH SERIES No 5

Evaluation: a key tool for improving drug prevention

Papers from the second European conference on the evaluation of drug prevention, 'Evaluation: a key tool for improving drug prevention', held in Strasbourg, France, from 2 to 4 December 1999.

PLANNING GROUP

Margareta Nilson
Gregor Burkhart
Sofia Feteira
Catherine Menier
Philippe Roux
Ulrik Solberg

EDITORIAL GROUP

Rachel Neaman
Margareta Nilson
Ulrik Solberg

EUROPEAN COMMISSION

E.M.C.D.D.A.
European Monitoring Centre for Drugs and Drug Addiction

Coordinated and compiled by Ulrik Solberg, European Monitoring Centre for Drugs and Drug Addiction (EMCDDA).

Detailed information on the EMCDDA and its work can be found on its website **(http://www.emcdda.org)**.

A great deal of additional information on the European Union is available on the Internet.
It can be accessed through the Europa server (http://europa.eu.int).

Cataloguing data can be found at the end of this publication.

Luxembourg: Office for Official Publications of the European Communities, 2000

ISBN 92-9168-105-9

Printed in Belgium

Contents

PART IV: RECOMMENDATIONS AND EVALUATION

PREFACE

This monograph contains the papers presented at the second European conference on the evaluation of drug prevention, 'Evaluation: a key tool for improving drug prevention', held in Strasbourg, France, from 2 to 4 December 1999. In addition to the conference papers, the volume includes the recommendations drawn up and adopted by the participants as the final outcome of the meeting. No conference on the theme of evaluation would be credible without itself being assessed, and this monograph also presents the results of an evaluation both of the event as a whole and of its individual workshop sessions.

The conference was organised jointly by the European Monitoring Centre for Drugs and Drug Addiction (EMCDDA) and the European Commission, a partnership that demonstrates the very real importance attached to evaluation in Europe today. The meeting brought together 160 participants from the EU Member States, central and eastern Europe, Canada, Chile, Iceland, Liechtenstein, Norway and the United States, as well as representatives from the Pompidou Group of the Council of Europe, the World Health Organisation and the United Nations International Drug Control Programme.

At the first European conference on the evaluation of drug prevention, held in Lisbon in March 1997, the EMCDDA presented its first tool designed specifically to facilitate this task, the *Guidelines for the evaluation of drug prevention* (1). This first conference highlighted the most common fears surrounding — and obstacles to — evaluation, and concluded that only by addressing these issues directly could resistance be overcome and an evaluation culture gradually introduced throughout the EU.

The meeting identified the major problems confronting evaluation as:

- lack of interest in the concept;
- fear or apprehension;
- lack of necessary skills;
- lack of resources.

Lack of interest

Evaluation involves clarifying and defining concepts and methods and assessing the impact of interventions. By examining these elements, diverse, unfocused activities prompted more by social anxieties than by genuine scientific research can be avoided and more efficient, targeted interventions introduced. Yet even today, three years after the first evaluation conference was held, the needs and objectives of drug-prevention programmes in Europe remain ill-defined. The large number of

(1) *Guidelines for the evaluation of drug prevention*, Manuals No 1, Lisbon, EMCDDA, 1998. A working document is also available to drug-prevention professionals in all 11 official EU languages directly from the EMCDDA.

requests the EMCDDA receives weekly for its evaluation guidelines from the EU Member States (over 1 500 working copies have been disseminated in all 11 official EU languages since 1997), however, demonstrates the growing interest of drug-prevention professionals in evaluation.

Fear or apprehension

Nevertheless, despite this growing interest in evaluation tools and methodologies, some of those responsible for implementing drug-prevention programmes are still unsure about the concept of evaluation. This reserve is undoubtedly linked to fear of the consequences of negative evaluation outcomes, since such results can lead to reductions in funding, whether from public or private sources. How to counter this problem was one of the main themes of this first conference.

Lack of necessary skills

Largely as a result of collaboration between national and European organisations, drug-prevention professionals now have far greater access to evaluation skills and examples of good practice. Among the materials and tools available are:

- the *Handbook prevention* of the Pompidou Group of the Council of Europe that details specific methodologies for devising drug-prevention interventions (2);
- the Evaluation of action against drug abuse in Europe (COST A-6) publication *Evaluation research in regard to primary prevention of drug abuse* that provides an overview of evaluation theory in Europe, clarifying specific concepts and terms (3);
- the EMCDDA's *Guidelines for the evaluation of drug prevention,* which complement the *Handbook prevention* and facilitate the planning and evaluation of drug-prevention interventions;
- the EMCDDA's Evaluation instruments bank (EIB), a database of tools to support professionals involved in evaluation (4);
- the EMCDDA's Exchange on drug demand-reduction action (EDDRA) on-line information system, which provides details of demand-reduction projects and evaluation methodology in the EU (5). EDDRA is also an educational and training tool which helps practitioners in the field to describe and document programme design.

There is now a real need to increase both the promotion and the acceptance of these tools at EU level as well as to continue to develop and improve them.

---

(2) Van der Stel, J. (Ed.) (1998), *Handbook prevention: alcohol, drugs and tobacco,* Strasbourg, Pompidou Group of the Council of Europe.

(3) Springer, A., Uhl, A. (Eds) (1998), *Evaluation research in regard to primary prevention of drug abuse,* Brussels, European Commission.

(4) For more on the EIB, see Chapter 6.

(5) For more on EDDRA, see Chapters 11 and 12. EDDRA is available at (http://www.emcdda.org/databases/databases_eddra.shtml).

Lack of resources

The evaluation tools developed by the EMCDDA and other organisations are mainly designed for use in internal evaluations, since evaluations by external institutions tend to be cost-intensive. Yet even in internal evaluations, the costs of allocating the necessary human resources have to be considered. It has been demonstrated, however, that the more evaluation is integrated into a programme, the lower the tangible costs and the higher the benefits in terms of continuous improvement. To this end, there is clearly a need to increase communication with public and private funding bodies to convince them of the value of investing in evaluation.

It has become evident via the EDDRA information system and through feedback from the focal points of the Reitox network (6) as well as from drug-prevention professionals that it is through practical experience that the feasibility of evaluation — even under difficult conditions or at a modest level, and at any stage of a project — must be demonstrated. This cannot only be done at scientific conferences and through journal articles, but also requires practical tools and advice to be made easily accessible.

Target groups

In addressing the four problem areas identified by the first evaluation conference, the second European conference on the evaluation of drug prevention was targeted above all at the 'users' of evaluations — the drug-prevention professionals responsible for implementing specific initiatives and the political decision-makers responsible for allocating funding — rather than at scientific evaluation experts.

This focus was intended to demonstrate that evaluation should not be seen as a form of control, but rather as a means of improving practice. In this context, results of less successful interventions play just as significant a role in improving and guiding future programmes as results of more successful projects. Qualitative data and process information, together with proper needs assessment, are as valuable for good evaluation practice as quantitative outcome results.

The need to allay fears of the consequences of negative evaluation outcomes must be balanced by the equal need to ensure that resources are allocated rationally. Priority should be given to drug-prevention projects that include both needs assessment and evaluation. Evaluation can facilitate the planning and design of drug-prevention programmes at local and regional level by establishing quality criteria which are not only based on outcomes. In this way, projects with adequate operational approaches but initially negative outcomes would not be automatically abandoned but would instead be reoriented. This concept of reorientation is crucial and the fact that negative evaluation outcomes are as important as positive ones should be a guiding principle of drug-prevention efforts.

(6) Reitox is the European information network on drugs and drug addiction and is coordinated by the EMCDDA in Lisbon. The network consists of a national focal point in each EU Member State, a focal point at the European Commission and an observer focal point in Norway.

Developing an evaluation culture

Given the current low level of drug-prevention evaluation in Europe, an EU-wide evaluation culture can only develop if programme designs are logical and coherent and thus lend themselves more easily to evaluation rather than focusing primarily on scientific demands. In the long term, and to ensure that evaluation is implemented as broadly as possible, including basic evaluation theory and knowledge in daily programme practice should be promoted and unrealistic expectations as to their impact avoided. In this context, the EMCDDA's *Guidelines for the evaluation of drug prevention* do not profess to be the ultimate guide to comprehensive evaluation research, but cover just one of several possible evaluation procedures.

Feedback from the field

To correct one frequent misconception, the EMCDDA's evaluation guidelines and tools deliberately do not mention specific theories, approaches and concepts since the Centre is not in a position to judge the theoretical foundations of all the diverse drug-prevention programmes currently implemented in Europe. Equally, the EMCDDA's tools should not be seen as European 'directives'. Instead, they are intended purely as a guide for improving practice and the Centre relies on feedback from drug-prevention professionals to improve and further develop these tools.

Another theme of the second European conference was therefore to adapt the EMCDDA's strategies more adequately to the problems encountered in evaluation. Cultural issues play an important role in this context, and in some Member States, initiatives are already under way to adapt the *Guidelines for the evaluation of drug prevention* — as well as drug-prevention programmes instituted in other countries — to different cultures of scientific thinking and understanding, as well as to specific national conditions.

Evaluation and the European Union

The European Commission is playing a crucial role in promoting evaluation. This is reflected not only in the fact that it co-organised the second European conference on the subject, but also in its commitment to spreading the culture of evaluation to all European drug-prevention activities.

The concept of evaluation lies at the heart of the first Community action programme for the prevention of drug dependence, which identifies data, research and evaluation as the primary areas for action (7). In this context, the programme foresees the recourse to EMCDDA information and to the possibilities offered by the EU Treaty to facilitate greater understanding of drugs and drug addiction at European Union level.

---

(7) Information on the Community action programme for the prevention of drug dependence is available at (http://europa.eu.int/comm/health/ph/programmes/drugs/index_en.htm).

It should be noted that, since 1998, completing the EDDRA reporting questionnaire has been an integral contractual requirement for the drug-prevention projects supported by the European Commission ([8]). The Commission also used the EMCDDA's evaluation guidelines and tools during its third European Drug Prevention Week held in November 1998.

The European Union Drugs Strategy (2000–04), approved at the December 1999 European Council meeting in Helsinki, envisages evaluation of all the programmes and policies it includes as a core task, another clear indication of the Commission's commitment to establishing a European-wide evaluation culture. In this context, the recommendations of the second European conference on the evaluation of drug prevention included in this monograph will no doubt play a central role both for the EMCDDA and for the European institutions in general.

I would like to extend my thanks and appreciation to all the conference speakers and workshop leaders whose thoughtful and stimulating presentations make up this monograph. I would also like to express my gratitude to the staff of the EMCDDA's Department of Drug-demand Reduction — particularly Margareta Nilson, Gregor Burkhart, Sofia Feteira, Catherine Menier, Philippe Roux and Ulrik Solberg — who organised the conference so ably and professionally, and to the SVA Travel SA which arranged the practical and logistical aspects of the conference with such efficiency. Finally, I would like to single out the efforts of Ulrik Solberg in coordinating the work of shaping the diverse elements of the second European conference on the evaluation of drug prevention into the coherent whole that is this monograph.

Georges Estievenart
Executive Director
EMCDDA

([8]) For details of the EDDRA questionnaire, see Chapters 11 and 12.

FOREWORD

The partnership between the European Commission and the European Monitoring Centre for Drugs and Drug Addiction — reflected both in their joint organisation of the second European conference on the evaluation of drug prevention and in their mutual commitment to spreading the culture of evaluation at EU level — is a crucial one.

The Commission's October 1999 interim report [9] on three of its Community action programmes in the field of public health — those targeting AIDS, cancer and drug dependence — presents the findings of an external evaluation by independent experts of the activities undertaken by these programmes [10]. The report specifically analyses the consistency, complementarity and effectiveness of the programmes and assesses the extent to which they have achieved their objectives.

A number of the initiatives set up in the framework of these action programmes have produced quite impressive results, with many of the multinational networks and teams that run them providing cost-effective added value to the European Community as a whole. Yet despite these positive developments, the project reports often fail to draw a convincing picture of their ability to obtain the necessary expertise and experience from all the EU Member States as well as to disseminate information on their activities effectively. The progressive use of electronic-information channels is, nevertheless, helping to counter this problem.

The projects in the public-health programmes are increasingly emphasising approaches targeted directly at individuals, and projects with a broad public policy approach are lacking. Furthermore, links between the drug-related projects and the Commission's other public-health programmes appear to be weak. This is particularly problematic given the new competency of the European Commission in the public-health field following the entry into force on 1 May 1999 of the Treaty of Amsterdam [11].

The importance and impact of this new treaty cannot be over-emphasised. While reiterating the importance of the health aspects of the drugs phenomenon, Article 152 (formerly Article 129) on public health recognises that health is a major issue relevant to a wide cross-section of Community policies and States:

> *A high level of human health protection shall be ensured in the definition and implementation of all Community policies and activities. … The Community shall complement the Member States' action in reducing drugs-related health damage, including information and prevention.*

---

(9) COM(1999) 463 final, 14.10.1999.

(10) Information on the Community action programmes in the field of public health is available at (http://europa.eu.int/comm/health/index_en.html).

(11) The text of the Treaty of Amsterdam is available on-line (http://europa.eu.int/eurlex/en/treaties/dat/ams_treaty_en.pdf).

This obligation is unique in introducing a quasi-constitutional requirement for the Community to take into account the possible health implications of its policy measures and actions. Such an obligation would also apply to the Community action plan for the fight against drugs of which the action programme for the prevention of drug dependence forms an integral part.

The European Commission is now considering developing an overall action plan in the field of public health, and has requested that the action programme for the prevention of drug dependence be extended to 2002 in the meantime.

Issues relating to reducing the demand for drugs, including doping in sports, remain a key priority for the European Commission. As a result, it is drawing on the recommendations made by the second European conference on the evaluation of drug prevention as a basis for a formal political proposal stressing the importance of appropriate evaluation of demand-reduction interventions in Europe.

Alexandre Berlin
Honorary Director of the European Commission representing Dr W. J. Hunter
Directorate-General F, Health and Consumer Protection

GENERAL INTRODUCTION

GENERAL INTRODUCTION

Margareta Nilson

The second European conference on the evaluation of drug prevention, 'Evaluation: a key tool for improving drug prevention', was both a follow-up to the first European conference on the evaluation of drug prevention, held in Lisbon in March 1997, and a unique event in its own right ([12]). Whereas the first conference had focused on the scientific aspects of evaluating drug prevention, the second conference concentrated rather on the practical and political aspects of evaluation.

Evaluation is an integral part of the European Union Drugs Strategy (2000–04) and an essential tool of the Community action programme for the prevention of drug dependence. In this context, the second European conference aimed:

- to demonstrate to both drug-prevention professionals and policy-makers how evaluation theory and knowledge can be implemented in practice;
- to promote an evaluation culture in Europe with a view to improving drug-prevention practice;
- to present practical experiences of the EMCDDA's evaluation tools — the *Guidelines for the evaluation of drug prevention,* the Evaluation instruments bank (EIB) and the Exchange on drug demand-reduction action (EDDRA) information system ([13]).

The conference was organised into four plenary sessions — with questions or comments after each presentation — and six workshops which were introduced by the session leader before opening up into a general discussion. While some of the speakers looked back and highlighted the developments that had taken place since the first evaluation conference, others addressed current and future issues and problems.

The EMCDDA: promoting the evaluation of drug prevention

The EMCDDA has implemented a number of initiatives to promote the evaluation of drug prevention. The most obvious example is its *Guidelines for the evaluation of drug prevention,* a manual targeted at programme planners and evaluators which includes checklists for planning and implementing evaluation as well as a series of practical examples.

([12]) The papers presented at the first European conference are available in *Evaluating drug prevention in the European Union*, Scientific Monograph No 2, Lisbon, EMCDDA, 1998.

([13]) For more on the *Guidelines for the evaluation of drug prevention*, see Chapters 5 and 6. For more on the Evaluation instruments bank, see Chapter 6. For more on the EDDRA system, see Chapters 11 and 12.

The second example of the EMCDDA's promotion of evaluation is its scientific monograph, *Evaluating drug prevention in the European Union,* which contains the presentations from the first European conference on the evaluation of drug prevention. The contributions range from studies of different phases of the evaluation process to epidemiological and cost-effectiveness issues.

The EMCDDA's two on-line databases — EDDRA and the EIB — provide information, respectively, on European drug demand-reduction activities that include an evaluation component, and on the tools used in such evaluations. EDDRA has been accessible on-line since 1998 ([14]), and a prototype of the EIB was demonstrated for the first time to the participants at the second conference on the evaluation of drug prevention. The Evaluation instruments bank will be accessible via the EMCDDA website during 2000.

Evaluating drug prevention has also been covered in EMCDDA publications such as *New trends in synthetic drugs in the European Union, Outreach work among drug users in Europe* and in the Centre's *Annual reports on the state of the drugs problem in the European Union* ([15]).

Purpose of the monograph

This volume is both a complement to the EMCDDA's second scientific monograph, *Evaluating drug prevention in the European Union,* and represents a significant step forward in promoting cooperation in the continuous effort to improve drug-prevention strategies and their evaluation in Europe.

A common question in drug prevention is 'what works?', and the chapters in this monograph, each from its own specific angle, attempt to address this central question. While the views expressed do not lead to a definitive or unambiguous answer, they do facilitate a better understanding of this complex field.

This monograph should not, however, be viewed as yet another attempt at EU harmonisation but, on the contrary, as a forum in which different players share their experiences and adapt their knowledge to different national contexts. Nor should this volume be seen as a definitive and final outcome of the second evaluation conference, but rather as one result of the process of improving drug prevention and its evaluation which will encourage and stimulate others in a 'ripple' effect for some time to come. The EMCDDA sees itself very much as a mediator in such efforts.

([14]) The EDDRA information system is available at (http://www.emcdda.org/databases/databases_eddra.shtml).

([15]) *New trends in synthetic drugs in the European Union*, Insights No 1, Lisbon, EMCDDA, 1997; *Outreach work among drug users in Europe*, Insights No 2, Lisbon, EMCDDA, 1999; *Annual report on the state of the drugs problem in the European Union*, Lisbon, EMCDDA, 1995, 1997, 1998, 1999.

Structure of the monograph

The monograph is divided into four parts. The first three parts follow the structure of the conference, while the fourth part presents the recommendations adopted at the end of the conference and the evaluation of the meeting itself.

- Part 1, 'Recent progress in evaluation', describes new developments in evaluation practice and how assessing programmes has helped to improve drug-prevention practice.
- Part 2, 'Improving drug-prevention practice', provides examples of actions which have led to better drug-prevention practice and describes the instruments and tools involved in the process.
- Part 3, 'Improving evaluation practice', analyses the obstacles that might impede or weaken the evaluation process, such as communication problems between evaluators and researchers, on the one hand, and policy-makers, on the other, or relations between the central, regional and local levels of government.
- Part 4, 'Recommendations and evaluation', concludes the monograph and includes the recommendations agreed by the conference participants. Given that one of the principal aims of the meeting was to promote evaluation through concrete examples, both the event itself and the individual workshop sessions were subject to a formal assessment. The findings of these evaluations are presented in this final section.

While this monograph can be read consecutively from beginning to end, the chapters can equally be referred to individually. It is hoped that the information it contains will be both useful and stimulating for decision-makers and drug-prevention professionals alike.

Recent progress in evaluation

Part I

Introduction

In Chapter 1, Jacques A. Bury explains why evaluation is so important. He explores its role, characteristics and utility, justifying its place as an indispensable element of drug prevention. The author examines the potential confrontation between political agendas and evaluation results and presents the criteria that future drug-prevention assessments will have to meet in order to overcome such obstacles.

Mark Morgan examines some of the factors associated with unsuccessful outcomes of drug-prevention programmes, as highlighted by recent research. Among the issues he discusses in Chapter 2 are the significance of cultural factors in designing drug-prevention interventions, the value of fear-arousal messages and the long-term effects of programmes that were not always evident at the time they were evaluated.

In Chapter 3, Tom Bucke explores how evaluation has successfully helped to shape drug-prevention practice by examining three recent case studies from the United Kingdom. These examples cover drug education in schools, prevention initiatives targeted at groups vulnerable to drug use, and drug prevention in the criminal-justice system.

Manuel Araujo Gallego takes the example of the Galician plan on drugs in Chapter 4 to highlight the impact of evaluation on regional drug-prevention policies. He examines how needs assessment can guide the equitable allocation of resources for drug prevention and describes the evaluation systems used by the plan on drugs. He concludes that for drug-prevention professionals, evaluation is the best way of improving both practice and policy and not an excuse for reducing budgets.

CHAPTER 1

EVALUATION: A KEY TOOL FOR IMPROVEMENT?

Jacques A. Bury

Whether or not evaluation is a key tool for improving drug prevention depends above all on the relationship between evaluation and the policies underlying specific prevention programmes.

Programme policies

The policies behind drug-prevention programmes vary depending on the way these programmes are devised and implemented. The policy is therefore determined by decision-making processes at different levels and how these processes take into account evaluation findings. In this context, it should be acknowledged that the administrative culture is not the most open to evaluating its practices.

In addition, the cultural differences between EU Member States — particularly between northern and southern Europe — cannot be ignored and indeed were explicitly recognised during a European symposium on evaluation in health education organised by the Collège Rhône-Alpes d'éducation pour la santé (CRAES) in Bordeaux in 1986. While these cultural differences may be becoming less marked, they do still remain — in EU parlance, there is 'convergence', but not 'harmonisation'.

Inspections and audits do not generally facilitate constructive dialogue for improving services. Instead, these practices are often associated with negative consequences such as staff changes or budgetary cuts. As a result, teams tend to hide the weak points of their programmes, thus preventing them from being addressed and improved.

What is evaluation?

Any human activity is evaluated — 'I breathe, therefore I evaluate' — and drug-prevention programmes are no exception. These assessments, however, generally remain anecdotal or implicit and thus may hamper more official evaluations, particularly in the way these are requested and interpreted. To some evaluators, the most important aspect of the process is, therefore, to make previously implicit judgments explicit.

A formal evaluation can be represented as the result of a decision made by X for official reasons Y and unofficial reasons Z. This co-existence of official and unofficial motives explains why many evaluators attach so much importance to clarifying the reason for the evaluation request as the preliminary stage of the process. An evaluation may, for example, be carried out in a bid to improve a specific programme, to justify it or prior to its cancellation. The assessment may be purely a formality and its findings never used, or may be requested after the basic programme decisions have already been taken.

In this chapter, evaluation is discussed in terms of its potential for improving drug-prevention programmes rather than from other perspectives, such as its role in increasing knowledge (evaluation research), controlling expenditure (auditing) or ensuring the smooth running of services (inspection). While there are literally hundreds of definitions of the term, each highlighting a particular aspect, the following interpretation reflects the 'utilitarian' purpose of evaluation: 'Evaluation is a process by which useful information for making helpful decisions is defined, obtained, analysed and provided'.

In this context, it is important to understand the mechanisms that influence what changes, if any, are made to a programme as a result of its evaluation. This involves identifying the respective roles played by the decision-makers (political or administrative), the drug-prevention professionals (who are paid by the programmes) and the target audience (which may provide direct feedback to the programme team or indirect feedback via public opinion or the media).

A recent report (Conseil Scientifique de l'Evaluation, 1996) illustrates that policies, as well as the programmes created to implement them, are always 'theoretical structures in the sense that they involve an a priori representation of the measures implemented, the attitude of the parties involved, the sequence of mechanisms for action and the resulting effects'. In reality, things never go according to plan. The parties involved in a drug-prevention programme may be forced to make unexpected decisions, either because practice never corresponds exactly to theory or because of the influence of personal ethics or interests.

It is generally accepted that evaluation should assess as objectively as possible the effects of a policy or programme, the ways in which it operates and the extent to which it achieves its objectives. 'As objectively as possible' implies both a certain distance — at least from those directly involved in the evaluation — and rigorous methods for carrying out and clarifying the specific approach taken.

The initial objectives of the evaluation are often reinterpreted or reformulated during the process. The inevitable difference between the official reasons for the evaluation and those interpreted by the person who commissioned it should not be underestimated. The official objectives are set out in a policy document, yet the original idea on which this document is based is almost always subject to selective, ad hoc and possibly inconsistent changes during the approval process. The official objectives are then in turn reinterpreted by the sponsor, who may have different ideas from the person who initiated the programme, who has himself changed since it was first devised, and so on.

Evaluation standards, elements and criteria

According to the *Petit guide de l'évaluation des politiques publiques* (Conseil Scientifique de l'Evaluation, 1996), successful evaluations fulfil many functions, including:

- a 'code-of-practice' role in providing a sense of accountability and demonstrating the need for transparency;
- a management role at micro level;
- a decision-making role at macro level;
- a didactic and motivational role for the parties directly involved.

Many standards have influenced evaluation practice, among them those of the Joint Committee on Standards for Educational Evaluation founded in 1975 in the United States ([16]). This committee has defined 30 norms which can be grouped into four categories:

- criteria of usefulness to guarantee that an evaluation meets the needs of its beneficiaries;
- feasibility criteria to ensure that an evaluation is realistic and cost-effective;
- code-of-practice criteria to demonstrate that an evaluation is conducted within the law, with respect for professional ethics and takes into account the well-being of those involved in the evaluation process, as well as those affected by its results;
- criteria of accuracy to guarantee that an evaluation uses information that is technically appropriate to the subject studied.

Evaluation also has political and technical aspects: politically, it provides the basis for informed decision-making or 'evidence-based public health'; technically, it can help to improve the effectiveness of drug-prevention programmes — hence the advantage, if not actually the obligation, for evaluators to study previous reports on all, or part, of the programme. The importance of this fundamental aspect is often underestimated.

Evaluation does not, however, provide the 'truth' about a programme, but is just one interpretation among many. The existence of different assessments of the same programme allows evaluators to gauge whether or not the institution managing the programme is able or willing to take into account the results of previous evaluations. It also allows the institution to reinforce particular recommendations by repeating them in the report. More generally, repeated evaluations can help to draw up guidelines for health-prevention and health-promotion initiatives. In this way, a significant reservoir of knowledge can be gradually built up, mainly through meta-analyses.

([16]) For more on the Joint Committee, see (http://www.eval.org/EvaluationDocuments/standards.html).

For evaluation research, and each individual evaluation, to be of value, its inevitable limitations must be clarified. The Conseil Scientifique de l'Evaluation (1996) states that the assessment process itself must be transparent:

> *As well as the demand for a full and rigorous statement of the methods used, this criterion includes the idea that the evaluation must contain an explanation of its approach and limitations. These are: its position in relation to other possible evaluations of the same subject; a reminder of issues to which it has not, or has not fully, responded; anticipation of possible objections, and so on. This attempt to think clearly and reflectively is even more necessary given that evaluations are generally imperfect, deliberately vague about certain issues and the results they achieve do not all have the same scope or strength.*

The evaluation programme or system adopted must balance the need for rigorous methods with the constraints — particularly in terms of time and resources — imposed by the given situation. As a rough guide, the evaluation budget should be between 2 and 15 % of the overall programme budget, depending on the time and resources available. The more innovative or visible the programme, the more thorough the evaluation must be. One of the most common ways of sabotaging an evaluation is to deliberately under-budget it.

'Time' here refers both to the time required to carry out the evaluation and to the time available on the sponsor's decision-making timetable. Since the two often conflict, this aspect should be negotiated. It is never easy to harmonise the evaluation timescale with the shelf-life of a policy. In an ideal system, the most important political decisions should be subject to a concomitant *ex ante* evaluation and an *ex post* appraisal of the objectives and methods. In practice, the consequences of an evaluation are often indirect and take a long time to appear. Experience tends to prove that the accumulated stock of studies and evaluations on a given issue, when this exists, is a permanent source that can be mobilised at any time, and for years, in informing decisions. However, the funds available tend to be scarce.

The case of the Cochrane Collaboration for evidence-based medicine is an inspiring example of such mechanisms, despite the arguable limitations of its methods. The Copenhagen-based European Observatory on Health Care Systems is another, as is the work carried out by the International Union for Health Promotion and Education (IUHPE, 1999a, 1999b) with help from the European Commission ([17]). The European Monitoring Centre for Drugs and Drug Addiction (EMCDDA) also contributes significantly to this structure, as does the European Commission's excellent guide to evaluation methods (European Commission, 1997).

Commissioning an evaluation inevitably requires terms of reference and/or a call for tender. It is clearly essential for the sponsors of the evaluation to know what they are

---

([17]) For more information on the Cochrane Collaboration, see (http://hiru.mcmaster.ca/cochrane/). For more information on the European Observatory on Health Care Systems, see (http://www.observatory.dk). For more information on the IUHPE, see (http://www.iuhpe.nyu.edu/).

requesting and they must thus have a realistic idea of what is desirable and possible given both the objectives and the constraints. The sponsor's knowledge in assessing the quality-to-price ratio of the tenders received is at least variable, not to say unpredictable. A consultant is seldom approached at this level, and yet a short feasibility study of the evaluation to help in planning its mandate and the terms of reference, as well as information on the budget required, would often help all those involved.

A distinction is generally made between policy evaluation and programme evaluation. The former is wider, both in terms of the field covered and the time required, and involves systematically assessing the programmes which are used to implement that policy. Evaluating overall programmes is more targeted and more easily understood by all actors, and must include a way of appraising the individual projects within the programme. The time required for the preliminary analysis, the collection of information and its assessment is one of the main differences between policy and programme evaluation; the effects on the evaluation budget is another.

A further distinction is also usually made between evaluating processes — continuing evaluation — and evaluating results — final evaluation. These can be categorised as either *ex ante* or a priori evaluation and *ex post* or a posteriori evaluation. *Ex ante* or a priori evaluation involves a long-term feasibility study and review of the impact of a particular measure. Where the measure involves a series of projects, the a priori evaluation is often associated with a process for selecting the best projects. In addition, if the evaluation results are made available to the managing body, they can also directly help to improve current or future projects. *Ex post* or a posteriori evaluation aims to provide retrospective information on a policy which has realised its full potential and become routine or on a completed programme. It is therefore a continuing, concomitant or 'as-you-go' evaluation.

It is perhaps more productive, however, to consider evaluation in terms of mechanistic and systematic approaches. The mechanistic approach explores the extent to which specific objectives are achieved, while the systematic approach considers the programme in the context of its environment. This method attempts to understand how the programme operates, the factors that facilitate it and those that render it more complicated, as well as identifying any unexpected effects — particularly over and above the specific objectives — and any limitations in its field of coverage. How should the managing body respond if the programme's mechanisms do not cover the planned field in its entirety? For example, are health-promotion projects included in drug-prevention programmes or not?

Linked to the mechanistic–systematic distinction is the distinction between the quantitative and qualitative schools of thought, which, in turn, is related to the concepts of objectivity and subjectivity. Supporters of the quantitative approach argue that what cannot be measured is not worth evaluating, whereas those who defend the qualitative approach argue that if it can be measured, it is probably of no interest (Chronbach, 1977; Davidson 1980). In fact, the multiplicity of information sources and the diversity of approaches introduces 'inter-subjectivity', which is perhaps the best form of relevant objectivity. But the diversity of evaluators also raises the issue of their technical reliability and of the greater risks of one of them failing (this risk is estimated at 10 %).

Internal and external evaluations

From the arguments in favour of an external evaluator, Nadeau (1981) cites:

- greater objectivity;
- ability to include evaluation criteria concerning the basic organisational premises;
- the possibility of acting as a mediator if internal disputes arise;
- a better protected status;
- greater ease in avoiding undesirable tasks which are not part of the evaluation.

From the arguments in favour of an internal evaluator, he cites:

- greater ability to develop detailed knowledge of the organisation and its programmes;
- a better position from which to carry out the continuing evaluation.

Most of the parties involved in evaluation increasingly accept the benefits of a functional relationship between an internal and external assessor. This will become increasingly natural as quality-assurance practices develop within training institutions, because the person responsible for these practices will often actually be the designated partner of the external evaluator.

In reality, however, the position of the internal assessor may be very delicate. The wider the gap between the unofficial and official reasons for the evaluation request, the more critical the position of the internal assessor, who is often as aware of the unofficial motives as of the official ones.

In the context of European drug-prevention programmes, an essential element for evaluation is one of the general objectives of all these initiatives, and also one of the criteria for selecting the individual projects within them: added Community value and its related issue of subsidiarity. These factors should also be among the criteria for choosing evaluators, both in terms of their knowledge of public health in the EU Member States and of European institutions.

What should guide both sponsors and evaluators is how useful the evaluation will be for improving the drug-prevention programme. It is essential that the sponsor in the formal sense, as well as the parties directly concerned — whether the main actors or the more remote decision-makers — can, in the end, adapt the results of the evaluation to drug-prevention practice. To do this, a certain number of conditions must be fulfilled. These include negotiating the evaluation contract as far as possible in consultation with all parties concerned, and undertaking to distribute the evaluation report immediately to everyone, even if this means accompanying it with a comment from the official sponsor specifying his own position. A not inconsiderable factor is the tone of the report, which often reflects the general atmosphere in which the evaluation has taken place. Clear criticism can be expressed by using measured, unemotional language.

Two factors, therefore, seem particularly important.

- The first is the evaluation process itself: the way in which the contract is negotiated and the interviews conducted with the parties involved, including the stance or code of ethics the assessor adopts.
- The second concerns the evaluation report, which, for many, is what finally remains of the evaluation. While answering the questions raised by the sponsor, the report must also include the points made along the way by all parties. It must above all be relevant to decision-making.

The evaluation report is a method of communication, not an academic thesis for the assessors nor a profitable investment for the sponsors. It is thus important to produce several versions of the same evaluation results targeted at the different audiences, whether decision-makers, drug-prevention professionals or the general population.

Formulating recommendations is a major component of the report and these must be supported by legitimate, comprehensible and credible arguments. It would, however, be dangerous if all the recommendations were systematically applied, since this would probably indicate that they had not been sufficiently considered. Conversely, it would be worrying if no recommendation were implemented. While it is unusual for evaluators to be formally associated with the decision-making resulting from their report, this would perhaps be the most effective solution if the majority of the recommendations were applied and if they were all consistent.

Conclusions

In conclusion, the following points should be borne in mind when planning and carrying out evaluations:

- results that arrive too late are useless;
- results that cannot be understood by the parties concerned are useless;
- results that cover minor, factual aspects are at best ineffectual, and at worst used improperly;
- (almost) everything depends on people: this is what tends to be evaluated the least, and taken into account even less.

References

Chronbach, J. L. (1977), 'Remarks to a new society', *Evaluation Research Society Newsletter*, No 1, pp. 1–3.

Conseil Scientifique de l'Evaluation (1996), *Petit guide de l'évaluation des politiques publiques*, Paris, La documentation française.

Davidson, P. (1980), 'Evaluating lifestyle change programs', in Davidson, P., Davidson, S., *Behavioural medicine: changing health lifestyles*, New York, Brunner/Mazel.

European Commission (1997), *Evaluating EU expenditure programmes: a guide.* Ex post *and intermediate evaluation,* Luxembourg, Office for Official Publications of the European Communities.

International Union for Health Promotion and Education (1999a), *The evidence of health promotion effectiveness: shaping public health in a new Europe.* A report for the European Commission by the International Union for Health Promotion and Education. Part 1, Core document, Luxembourg, Office for Official Publications of the European Communities.

International Union for Health Promotion and Education (1999b), *The evidence of health promotion effectiveness: shaping public health in a new Europe.* A report for the European Commission by the International Union for Health Promotion and Education. Part 2, Evidence book, Luxembourg, Office for Official Publications of the European Communities.

Nadeau, M. A. (1981), *L'évaluation des programmes d'études: théorie et pratique,* Quebec, Les presses de l'Université Laval.

Further reading

Campbell, G. (1984), *Health education and youth,* London and Philadelphia, Palmer Press.

Chapter 2

Evaluation and drug-prevention research: implications of unsuccessful outcomes for programme design

Mark Morgan

Over the past few years, increasing concerns have been raised about the need to design more effective programmes to combat drug use in Europe. The 1995 European schools project on alcohol and other drugs (ESPAD) study has demonstrated that, while differences exist between countries both in terms of the substances used and the age of onset of drug use, each of the countries and regions surveyed cited problems with either legal or illegal substances (Hibell et al., 1997) ([18]). The study also revealed a strong association between drug problems and crime, as well as a decline in gender differences in drug use, with use by girls tending to 'catch up' with boys in several countries (Hibell et al., 1997).

At the same time, the literature on the evaluation of drug-prevention efforts has frequently suggested that such programmes are either only moderately successful or downright failures (Brown and Kreft, 1998). Programmes may fail because:

- they are not properly implemented;
- the measures they adopt are too weak to change the target behaviour or attitude;
- there is no clear rationale for the intervention;
- they do not take into account the factors that underpin initiation to drug use.

This chapter examines some of the factors associated with unsuccessful outcomes of drug-prevention programmes that have emerged in recent research studies. Particular attention is paid to the importance of cultural factors in programme design, the value of messages focusing on risk, and the long-term effects of programmes which were not evident at the time of their evaluation.

The reason for examining these issues is twofold. First, despite the growing interest in drug-prevention programmes in Europe, the majority of evaluation studies come from the United States (Foxcroft, Lister-Sharp and Lowe, 1997), thus linking the accumulated wisdom to a specific cultural and economic context. Second, it is the author's conviction that drug-prevention efforts can be improved by broadening the

([18]) The countries or regions surveyed were Croatia, Cyprus, Czech Republic, Denmark, England, Estonia, Faeroe Islands, Finland, Hungary, Iceland, Ireland, Italy, Latvia, Lithuania, Malta, Northern Ireland, Norway, Poland, Portugal, Scotland, Slovakia, Slovenia, Sweden, Turkey, Ukraine and Wales.

frame of reference behind such programmes to socio-psychological models of influence and behavioural change.

Cultural-specific drug-prevention programmes

Many contemporary approaches to drug prevention are based on the assumption that young people may overestimate the level of social acceptance that exists for substance-use behaviour. It is thought that correcting such misperceptions reduces substance use because normative influences have a powerful impact on behaviour (Graham, Marks and Hansen, 1991). This raises the related issue of whether the frequency of alcohol and other drug use is, in fact, overestimated. The literature includes a phenomenon called the 'false consensus effect' — the belief by users of a particular drug that use by others is more frequent than it actually is. Conversely, those who are not themselves frequent users tend to see themselves as quite unique, thus leading to a general overestimation of actual use. This phenomenon has also been referred to as 'pluralistic ignorance' in some publications (Prentice and Miller, 1993).

The ESPAD study questioned more than 50 000 16-year-old students from 26 countries and regions. One of the survey questions required them to estimate the frequency of substance use by their friends.

In 20 countries, the frequency of smoking was overestimated. Interestingly, the six countries in which there was no such distortion — Denmark, Faeroe Islands, Finland, Iceland, Norway and Sweden — are both culturally and geographically linked. In these countries, there was either no substantial overestimation, or the percentage of young people who said that 'most or all' of their friends smoked was actually less than the percentage who had themselves reported smoking during the previous month.

The ESPAD study demonstrated even greater distortion in reports of drunkenness. In 20 of the 25 countries for which data were available, the percentage who reported drunkenness amongst 'most or all' of their friends was greater than the actual number who admitted such behaviour. More significantly, the countries where this effect was not evident were the same Nordic States where no major misrepresentation was evident in the case of smoking, with the exception of the Faeroe Islands.

There are a number of possible explanations for this interesting pattern. It may be that adolescents in most countries except the Nordic States underestimate their own substance use, or that such use may be more secretive and therefore less visible in Nordic countries. However, without further investigation, such interpretations are merely speculative.

The ESPAD findings have clear implications for the design of drug-prevention programmes and specifically for those that attempt to influence behaviour through norm correction. The study shows that while widespread overestimation of substance use is common, it is by no means universal. This raises the issue of whether a programme designed to correct misperceptions can be effective in cultures where no such misperception actually exists.

Fear-arousal messages

As has been proved by a long tradition in psychology, fear-arousal messages change behaviour. The basic assumption is that assimilating knowledge about the negative consequences of substance use reduces favourable attitudes towards it, which in turn decreases the likelihood of actual use. In particular, if the dangerous consequences of a given behaviour were to be spelled out graphically, then young people would avoid the behaviour in question. This view has led in certain circumstances, especially in the intervention programmes of the 1970s, to educators believing that exaggerating the consequences of drug use can be justified if it prevents young people from experimenting with drugs.

Table 1: Perceived risk of substance use

Country/region	20+ cigarettes daily	5+ drinks at weekends	Occasional marijuana use	Regular marijuana use	Occasional ecstasy use	Regular ecstasy use
Croatia	57	44	55	82	59	79
Cyprus	63	71	53	87	51	—
Czech Republic	75	39	37	78	47	80
Denmark	70	13	21	71	36	69
England	55	20	23	44	53	78
Estonia	71	38	44	78	29	55
Faeroe Islands	83	31	40	85	52	82
Finland	68	30	49	91	60	89
Hungary	77	55	62	89	60	86
Iceland	74	37	42	89	86	53
Ireland	61	16	19	57	45	81
Italy	63	33	49	83	58	85
Latvia	68	52	56	82	55	79
Lithuania	74	54	63	76	57	74
Malta	53	40	60	61	59	79
Northern Ireland	66	23	36	61	59	85
Norway	56	29	36	87	39	85
Poland	84	46	64	93	65	93
Portugal	69	53	67	89	69	90
Scotland	60	20	14	32	53	78
Slovakia	68	45	52	87	56	85
Slovenia	49	40	48	79	47	79
Sweden	65	45	52	92	58	91
Turkey	75	62	76	89	74	—
Ukraine	46	58	61	80	60	76
Wales	69	12	23	47	53	82

NB:
The figures shown are the percentage of respondents who believed that the behaviour in question was a 'great risk'.
'—' indicates data not available.
Source: Hibell et al., 1997.

However, there is now more than adequate evidence to refute this approach. In the ESPAD study, the issue of risk was addressed in two ways. First, the survey obtained information on the extent to which young people thought that substance use was indeed a serious danger. Second, these data were analysed across countries to see whether there was a correlation between the level of risk perception and the extent of reported substance use.

Table 1 above shows the percentage of respondents who believed that a certain substance-use behaviour was a 'great risk'. Each of the areas covered by the survey — heavy smoking, heavy drinking, occasional and regular use of cannabis and ecstasy — is of particular interest, for example in illustrating the success of campaigns to convince young people of the dangers of these behaviours.

Two points are especially noteworthy. First, a substantial minority in each country did not perceive that smoking 20 or more cigarettes daily was a 'great' risk, but thought it involved a 'slight', 'moderate' or 'no' risk. Thus, despite the extensive information campaigns conducted over the past decades, a great many young Europeans do not believe that heavy smoking is dangerous. In Ireland, Norway, Sweden and the UK (England, Northern Ireland, Scotland and Wales), where there have been sustained and intense anti-smoking campaigns, between one-third and two-fifths of young people were not convinced that smoking over 20 cigarettes a day was a great risk.

The second point concerns the differences in risk perception associated with occasional substance use (once or twice) and regular use. In every country, substantially more respondents thought that regular cannabis use was more dangerous than occasional use. This suggests that the critical feature in the perception of risk is not simply the substance, but its frequency of use. A broadly similar pattern was found in relation to ecstasy.

Also significant is the correlation between risk perception and actual drug use. In countries where a higher proportion of young people view use of a certain substance as risky, is its use relatively lower? The ESPAD study demonstrates that the association between risk perception and reported substance use depends on both the substance and the level of use involved. Thus, in the case of smoking, the correlation with lifetime smoking is neither substantial nor significant. These results imply that even if young people accept that smoking is dangerous, they may still take up the habit.

Two important findings emerge regarding risk perception and smoking. First, a substantial number of young Europeans do not accept that smoking is a 'great risk'. Second, in those countries where relatively more young people accept that smoking does pose a great risk, the prevalence of smoking is just as great (or even greater) than in countries where the risk perception is lower.

The association between perceived risk and prevalence is, however, much stronger and more negative in the case of both alcohol and illicit drugs. For alcohol, the correlations are negative but modest in relation to lifetime prevalence of drinking or previous-month drinking, but are stronger in relation to heavy drinking (actually being drunk). This reflects the fact that the risk measure used focuses on heavy drinking (five or more drinks) ([19]). Thus, it would seem that in those countries where young people accept that heavy drinking poses risks, they are less likely to get drunk.

In the ESPAD study, the perception of the risks posed by illicit substances was closely related to low levels of use. This was true for all four measures of risk (occasional and regular use of cannabis and occasional and regular use of ecstasy). Thus, perceived risk seems to have a quite different effect on actual use of cigarettes, alcohol and illicit substances: risk perception appears to play a negligible part in cigarette smoking, a significant part in heavy drinking and drunkenness and a major part in all aspects of drug use. While the ESPAD data do not allow firm conclusions to be extrapolated, it may not be coincidental that the risks of cigarette smoking are long term while those associated with heavy drinking and drug use also involve short-term hazards, such as personal injury ([20]).

Breadth of programme and outcome effectiveness

How appropriate is it to target one or several substances, or indeed to incorporate drug use into a comprehensive health-education programme? It would seem reasonable for drug-prevention programmes to target several substances at once. In addition, the rationale behind a particular drug-prevention programme may make it logical to incorporate several substances rather than a single one. A further practical reason is the clear limit to the number of discrete, special-purpose drug-prevention programmes that any system of delivery can accommodate before becoming redundant and unwieldy.

Some of the most promising evidence of the widespread effects of drug-prevention programmes comes from studies with schoolchildren. Frankel (1998) suggests that intensive drug-prevention intervention with pre-school children in early-childhood programmes could help decrease their drug use in adolescence. The long-term effects could be related to the degree to which parents are involved in drug-prevention interventions with their children.

In addition, it has been found that preventing poor academic performance among schoolchildren itself has a powerful effect on reducing substance misuse several years later. While early-childhood interventions such as Head Start — which was implemented throughout the United States in the 1960s — were designed to enhance school performance rather than to improve social behaviour or to prevent substance use at a later stage, such benefits have been demonstrated, possibly as a result of improved school performance and family relations. Programmes designed to enhance pupils' achievement in school have been shown to produce a range of social and personal effects which decreased anti-social behaviour in adolescence and beyond. Childhood programmes aimed at improving school performance are thus a viable way of decreasing juvenile delinquency (Lerner and Galambos, 1998).

([19]) Here, a drink is defined as a glass of wine, a bottle of beer, a small measure of spirits or a mixed drink.

([20]) For further discussion of the ESPAD survey results, see Morgan et al. (1999).

There are at least two explanations for this remarkable finding. One view suggests that cognitive development, including academic achievement, leads to greater success in — and commitment to — school and consequently to lower rates of delinquency. The HIGH SCOPE project implemented in several parts of the United States in the late 1960s in particular supports this hypothesis. Young children from disadvantaged backgrounds who participated in this essentially cognitively oriented programme demonstrated substantially lower rates of delinquency at age 15 than non-participants (31 % compared to 51 %), and this difference remained stable until young adulthood (Lerner and Galambos, 1998).

Another explanation relates to the family. There is evidence that early-childhood drug-prevention programmes improve family functioning, especially parenting skills and relations between the family and the school. Improved family functioning leads to more nurturing parenting which in turn reduces the risk of anti-social behaviour. For example, children who participated in a programme with both a school and a home component over five years had a much lower rate of delinquency than a control group in a 10-year follow-up (6 % compared to 22 % — Lerner and Galambos, 1998).

While most explanations of the link between intervention and preventing delinquency have to date been couched in terms of either 'cognitive advantage' or 'family support', additional factors are also likely to be involved. Positive effects on young people's self-concept, on their motivation or on their social development may provide crucial links between participating in a drug-prevention programme and its observed effects.

These findings have very significant implications for drug-prevention policies by providing a link with other initiatives in areas that are generally not considered to be relevant to substance use. They also present an opportunity for integrating research on substance-use prevention into research on other social issues, including educational disadvantage and poor school performance.

Conclusions

There is considerable evidence that drug-prevention programmes designed for use in all societies and cultures are likely to be difficult to develop and implement. The evidence of cultural influences on risk factors make this an important area for further study. The effect of gender and age differences may have a similar effect and equally require further investigation.

The data considered in this chapter, both from the ESPAD study and from other sources, indicate that emphasising the risks and dangers of substance use is of limited value as fear-arousal messages are not believed or, if they are, their capacity to influence behaviour is weak.

Similarly, how appropriate is it for drug-prevention programmes to target a single (or several) substances, and might it be better to broaden school drug-prevention programmes in other ways? Particularly interesting is the long-term value of efforts to prevent academic failure among schoolchildren, which have been shown also to affect social behaviour and subsequent drug use during adolescence.

References

Brown, J. H., Kreft, I. G. G. (1998), 'Zero effects of drug-prevention programs: issues and solutions', *Evaluation Review*, No 22, pp. 3–14.

Foxcroft, D. R., Lister-Sharp, D., Lowe, G. (1997), 'Alcohol misuse prevention for young people: a systematic review reveals methodological concerns and lack of reliable evidence of effectiveness', *Addiction*, No 92, pp. 531–37.

Frankel, A. J. (1998), 'The case for drug prevention in early childhood', *Alcoholism Treatment Quarterly*, No 16, pp. 13–23.

Graham, J. W., Marks, G., Hansen, W. B. (1991), 'Social influence processes affecting adolescent substance use', *Journal of Applied Psychology*, No 76, pp. 291–98.

Hibell, B., Andersson, B., Bjarnason, T., Kokkevi, A., Morgan, M., Narusk, A. (1997), *The ESPAD report: alcohol and other drug use among students in 26 European countries*, Stockholm, Swedish Council for Information on Alcohol and other Drugs.

Lerner, R. M., Galambos, N. L. (1998), 'Adolescent development: challenges and opportunities for research, programs and policies', *Annual Review of Psychology*, No 49, pp. 413–46.

Morgan, M., Hibell, B., Andersson, B., Bjarnason, T., Kokkevi, A., Narusk, A. (1999), 'The ESPAD study: implications for prevention', *Drugs, Prevention and Policy*, No 6, pp. 243–56.

Prentice, D. A., Miller, D. T. (1993), 'Pluralistic ignorance and alcohol use on the campus: some consequences of misperceiving the social norm', *Journal of Personality and Social Psychology*, No 64, pp. 243–56.

Further reading

Hansen, W. B. (1992), 'School-based substance abuse prevention: a review of the state of the art in curriculum, 1980–90', *Health Educational Research*, No 7, pp. 403–30.

Johnson, C. A., MacKinnon, D. P., Pentz, M. A. (1996), 'Breadth of program and outcome effectiveness in drug abuse prevention', *American Behavioural Scientist*, No 39, pp. 884–96.

Petraitis, J., Flay, B. R., Miller, T. Q. (1995), 'Reviewing theories of adolescent substance use: organising pieces of the puzzle', *Psychological Bulletin*, No 117, pp. 67–86.

CHAPTER 3

EVALUATION AND DRUG-PREVENTION PRACTICE: RECENT PROGRESS

Tom Bucke

In the middle of difficulty lies opportunity. (Albert Einstein)

Evaluation has not always had an easy relationship with drug policy and practice. Funds for drug-prevention evaluation have either not consistently been available or have not always been sufficient, and the effectiveness of various practices and policies have thus remained either unknown or unclear. Even when rigorous evaluations have been conducted, their findings (whether positive or negative) have at times been ignored by both policy-makers and practitioners. In addition, evaluators have been guilty of not producing policy- or practitioner-relevant findings or of not adequately communicating these findings to their audiences.

While acknowledging these problems, this chapter focuses on three case studies where evaluation has successfully helped to shape drug-prevention practice. Drawing on developments in the United Kingdom since the first European conference on the evaluation of drug prevention in 1997, these examples cover three very different areas of intervention:

- drug education in schools;
- 'vulnerable groups';
- the criminal-justice system.

Each of the interventions cited below took place in the context of the UK Government's 10-year plan targeting drug misuse ('Tackling drugs to build a better Britain', 1998). This plan set key performance targets for reducing drug use and led to extra funding for drug-related law enforcement, treatment and prevention. This, and other, government initiatives dealing with health, housing and educational inequalities place a high value on 'evidence-based practice' derived from rigorous evaluation. As a result, funders are increasingly looking at activities in the drug-prevention field and asking: are they effective?

Case study one: drug prevention and education

The first case study concerns primary drug prevention in schools. A significant amount of evaluation data is now available on what is effective in this area. For example, drug education has traditionally placed strong emphasis on providing young people with information on patterns of drug consumption, pharmacology, methods of using drugs and so on. This approach may also involve more emotive means, such as fear-arousal strategies that dramatise the negative effects of drug use and frighten young people into remaining abstinent. A central assumption underpinning these approaches is that if young people are informed about the dangers of drugs they will make a rational decision to avoid them.

Despite the widespread adoption of this approach, evaluations have demonstrated that providing information on drugs does not, by itself, have a significant impact on young peoples' drug use (Ellickson 1993; Dielman, 1994). This is not to say that providing information in drug education is pointless, but that to have a sustained impact on drug consumption, information and programmes that address young peoples' attitudes need to be coupled with psychological approaches. One of the most promising current psychological approaches in drug education is 'life-skills training' which seeks to develop generic, personal self-management and social skills. The aptitudes typically developed by this training include:

- decision-making and problem-solving;
- cognitive faculties for resisting interpersonal and media influences;
- capabilities for enhancing self-esteem;
- coping strategies for dealing with stress and anxiety;
- general social skills (complimenting, conversation and forming new friendships);
- general assertive techniques (including requests and refusals).

These generic skills are taught and applied to situations relating to tobacco, alcohol and drug use, although they could equally be applied to other areas, such as sexual behaviour and juvenile delinquency.

Life skills and 'Project Charlie'

The main evidence for life-skills training comes from North America and Australia (Wragg, 1990; Botvin et al. 1995) and shows significantly lower levels of cannabis, tobacco and alcohol use among young people who receive the training than among those who do not. Despite the existence of these studies, however, drug-educational practice in the UK for most of the 1990s remained uninformed by this evidence and continued to be variable in coverage, quality and approach. An exception was a life-skills programme called Project Charlie, initiated in 1992 in a deprived part of East London among a group of 5–11-year-olds ([21]). These children were assessed four years after the start of the project and compared to a control group who had not participated in the programme (Hurry and Lloyd, 1997).

([21]) Project Charlie — Chemical Abuse Resolution Lies in Education — was originally developed in the US to promote abstinence among schoolchildren, delay the onset of first experimentation with drugs, limit the amount, frequency and situations in which drug use occurs, and inhibit the further development of drug use.

The results of the evaluation showed that compared to the control pupils the Project Charlie children:

- were more resistant to peer pressure;
- exhibited more negative attitudes to drugs;
- were less likely to have used tobacco and illicit drugs.

While the Project Charlie evaluation was a modest study with a small sample size, the findings re-emerged in 1997 when the UK's 10-year drug strategy was being formulated. Senior policy-makers were looking for evidence of 'what worked' in drug education and the Project Charlie evaluation had a strong influence on their thinking. As a result, the UK's new drug strategy states that 'prevention should start early, with broad life-skills approaches' from ages 5 to 11. All schools in the UK are now expected to establish 'integrated, sustained and comprehensive programmes involving life-skills approaches' by 2002 (UK Anti-drugs Coordinator, 1999). Drug-prevention programmes outside schools involving young people and their parents are also to include life-skills approaches. Promoting life skills in school drug education, however, has implications for both funding and teacher training. New educational materials will need to be created or existing ones rewritten and the extent to which teachers apply the method across the UK monitored. One of the major lessons here is the opportunistic nature of research evaluation. The Project Charlie evaluation demonstrates how positive research findings, if they emerge at the right time for the right audience, can have a major impact on policy and practice.

Case study two: drug prevention and 'vulnerable groups'

The second case study concerns groups 'vulnerable' to problem drug use ([22]). Such users typically consume large amounts of heroin, crack or amphetamines, usually as part of a pattern of 'poly' drug use ([23]). Over recent years, research has led to the growing realisation that some young people are more likely to develop serious drug problems than others (Lloyd, 1998; Lloyd and Griffiths, 1998). To put it another way, those people who have serious drug problems often exhibit common life experiences, including dysfunctional family backgrounds and troubled school careers. As a result, vulnerable or high-risk groups tend to include those excluded from school, truants, children in care, young offenders, the young homeless and children of drug-misusing parents.

The growing awareness of vulnerability to problem drug use has occurred at a time of increasing interest across Europe in issues of social exclusion and marginalisation and how social disadvantage influences drug consumption among young people.

([22]) Problem drug use involves dependence, regular excessive use, or use that causes serious health issues. A distinction should be made between problem and casual or recreational drug users. For a more detailed definition of problem drug use, see Advisory Council on the Misuse of Drugs (1982, 1988).

([23]) 'Poly' drug use is a pattern of consumption that involves a number of licit and/or illicit drugs. Polydrug users would include a stimulant user who regularly smokes heroin in order to ease the after effects of using crack cocaine.

This perspective creates exciting possibilities for drug-prevention practice. If vulnerable young people can be identified at an early stage, then drug-prevention and harm-reduction activities could be more effectively targeted. This issue also raises a number of questions for practitioners, such as how to identify and access vulnerable groups and what prevention interventions should be delivered. Even if these questions can be answered, working with vulnerable young people is likely to be a challenging experience. While some groups may be physically accessible, their experiences and backgrounds may render them chaotic, inattentive and suspicious of authority.

Working with excluded schoolchildren

Griffiths et al. (1999) have addressed work with vulnerable young people in the UK by focusing on those expelled or excluded from school who have been grouped together in 'pupil referral units' (24). Because there is very little evidence on which approaches actually work with vulnerable groups, and in particular with excluded schoolchildren, the project workers had to design their own drug-prevention programme. This programme involved three elements.

- Drug education was delivered by outside facilitators in sessions that sought to ensure that the young people had a sound knowledge base for taking decisions on substance use. Topics covered included types of drugs, their effects and dangers, and drugs and the law.
- Life-skills training was provided through a specially developed course delivered by outside facilitators. This course sought to assist the young people in dealing with difficult situations and problems, and to enhance their communication skills and interaction with others.
- Diversionary activities of a vocational and educational nature were delivered throughout the programme. The nature of these activities was at the discretion of the individual pupil referral units.

Evaluation of this initiative began in 1997 and shows how research can shape and improve a drug-prevention intervention. For example, first-year research findings described how the diversionary element of the programme had been oversold. Not all units were providing these pursuits, and when they did these were not the intensive training or skill-based activities that had been originally planned. As a result of the evaluation, the package was modified and these shortcomings addressed.

Second-year research findings showed that the programme was well received by the young participants. The results specifically found that:

- just under one third stated that the course had actually changed their attitudes to drugs;

(24) Pupil referral units are specialised centres where young people continue their education after being permanently excluded from a number of schools. The units are locally based and run either by the local education authority or by a voluntary agency. The young people who attend these units tend to be aged 11 to 16.

- just over one third stated that they would be less likely to take drugs after attending the course.

While these are comparatively weak indicators of success ([25]), an evaluation report on the third year will present further findings on the outcome and impact of the programme on drug use. This report will be published in the latter half of 2000.

Case study three: drug prevention and the criminal-justice system

The third example of the impact of evaluation on drug-prevention practice concerns the increasing involvement of the criminal justice system in engaging problem drug users who are often extensively involved in crime to support their drug consumption.

The police and the courts are among the agencies that have the most contact with problem drug users. But while the criminal-justice system can apprehend and prosecute this population, there is little evidence that conviction and punishment do anything to reduce their substance use. By contrast, there is quite good evidence that properly funded and appropriately designed interventions by drug agencies can substantially reduce drug use and drug-related crime (Hough, 1996).

In the UK, this has led to various strategies to identify problem drug users in the criminal-justice system and refer them to specialised services for treatment. While these strategies do not fit neatly into traditional notions of drug prevention, when linked to treatment their objectives are to reduce drug use, drug-related harm and drug-related crime.

Problem drug users and 'arrest referral schemes'

One strategy that has recently been evaluated involves 'arrest referral schemes'. These schemes focus on people entering the criminal-justice system after arrest when they are in police custody. 'Arrest' means a break in offending, and in this context offers drug users a chance to reflect on their behaviour, in the context of possible prosecution and conviction.

Different types of arrest referral schemes have been evaluated with samples of arrestees monitored on referral to treatment agencies (Edmunds et al., 1998). Two of the main findings from the evaluation are described below.

Types of arrest referral scheme

Initially, a large number of arrest referral schemes were based on the 'information model' where police officers provide details of local drug agencies and treatment

([25]) Interventions that have successfully changed young peoples' attitudes and intentions towards drug use have not always been successful in changing their actual behaviour (Moshowitz, 1989).

services to all arrestees on a 'take-it-or-leave-it' basis. While these schemes are cheap to establish, they have very poor take-up rates.

A more effective approach in terms of participation by arrestees is the 'proactive model'. Under this model, drug workers cooperate closely with the police and often directly approach arrestees in custody, providing an assessment either on site or at a later meeting. In some cases, the police may screen or target arrestees for the drug worker, although the worker is always responsible for providing information about drug services and encouraging the user to seek advice.

Impact of arrest referral schemes

Those passing through these schemes tend to be white male opiate users in their late twenties or early thirties. They have a high weekly expenditure on drugs which they finance through shoplifting, burglary, selling drugs and a variety of other illegal and legal means. The evaluation found that three-quarters of those seen by drug workers were referred to drug services and half entered a treatment programme. Interviews up to 18 months after the first contact with the arrest referral scheme found that the participants' expenditure on drugs had fallen from GBP 375 per week (EUR 225) to GBP 70 (EUR 42). The greatest differences were reported among opiate and stimulant users. Corresponding decreases were found in levels of offending to finance drug use, while in terms of harm reduction, the prevalence and frequency of injecting had fallen.

The effect of the arrest referral evaluation on policy and practice has been enormous. The UK Government is currently looking at ways of reducing the impact of crime and drug misuse, and arrest referral schemes are seen as having the potential to make a real impact on these areas. The findings of the evaluation have led to GBP 20 million (EUR 12 million) being set aside to develop arrest referral schemes in every police station across the UK by 2002. This means a massive increase in the number of drug workers based in the criminal-justice system and the significant refocusing of UK drug-prevention practice. If these new arrest referral schemes succeed in engaging the numbers expected, drug agencies will have to expand to meet the numbers of new clients being referred to them. Part of the GBP 20 million will therefore be used to finance the extra drug services required to deal with the criminal-justice referrals.

Referral schemes are currently being evaluated in other parts of the criminal-justice system, including those attached to prisons, courts and 'community sentences'. If these schemes prove successful, they may lead to increased emphasis being placed on criminal justice in drug-prevention practice.

Conclusions

The importance of evaluation in drug prevention is increasing, reflecting a wider trend in social policy over the 1990s from 'inputs' to 'outputs'. In the past, policy-makers and practitioners addressed a particular social issue or problem by stating how much money had been spent, how many new posts had been created, or how much time had been given to it (inputs). This position is becoming increasingly hard to sustain. Instead, policy-makers and practitioners are now expected to provide evidence of what has been achieved by the money they have spent, the posts they have created and the time they have allocated (outputs). As a result of this change, policy-makers are increasingly looking to evaluators for assistance ([26]).

Three common themes run through the case studies outlined above. The first is that the impact of evaluation on drug-prevention practice may depend on timing. In other words, providing policy-makers with evidence of effectiveness when they need it can have a major effect on practice. The lessons here for evaluators include recognising the opportunities available to them to make an impact on practice, and marketing evidence of effectiveness in drug prevention in the most appropriate ways.

The second idea is that evaluations do not have to be large and resource-intensive to make an impact on practice. The Project Charlie evaluation was modest in size and budget but, because it confirmed international findings in a UK setting, its influence has been very significant. Taking examples of effective drug-prevention practice from the international literature and applying them to a specific country is one way of influencing practice. Again, a crucial element here is to recognise and seize opportunities when they arise.

The third theme is that negative evaluation findings can be just as valuable as positive ones. In each of the case studies outlined above, evaluation has highlighted approaches that did not work or were not very effective. Instead of being interpreted as 'prevention does not work', these results have led to drug-prevention practitioners developing more effective approaches and more effective evaluation practice.

References

Botvin, G. J., Baker, E., Dusenbury, L., Botvin, E. M., Diaz, T. (1995), 'Long-term follow-up results of a randomised drug abuse prevention trial in a white middle-class population', *Journal of the American Medical Association*, No 273, pp. 1106–112.

Dielman, T. E. (1994), 'School-based research on the prevention of adolescent alcohol use and misuse: methodological issues and advances', *Journal of Research on Adolescence*, No 4, pp. 271–93.

Edmunds, M., May, T., Hearnden, I., Hough, M. (1998), *Arrest referral: emerging lessons from research*, Drug Prevention Initiative Paper 23, London, Home Office Central Drug Prevention Unit.

Ellickson, P. L. (1993), 'Schools', in Coombs, R. H., Ziedonis, D. (Eds), *Handbook of drug abuse prevention*, Englewood Cliffs, NJ, Prentice Hall.

([26]) UK Government ministries now commonly allocate 10 to 15 % of a new initiative's budget to evaluation.

Griffiths, P., Powis, B., Khan-Lodhi, J. (1999), *Developing effective drug prevention for school excludees: discussion of emerging findings*, London, Home Office Drugs Prevention Advisory Service.

Hough, M. (1996), *Problem drug use and criminal justice: a review of the literature*, Drug Prevention Initiative Paper 15, London, Home Office Central Drug Prevention Unit.

Hurry, J., Lloyd, C. (1997), *A follow-up evaluation of Project Charlie: a life-skills drug education programme for primary schools*, Drug Prevention Initiative Paper 16, London, Home Office Central Drug Prevention Unit.

Lloyd, C. (1998), 'Risk factors for problem drug use: identifying vulnerable groups', *Drugs: Education, Prevention and Policy*, No 5, pp. 217–32.

Lloyd, C., Griffiths, P. (1998), 'Editorial: problems for the future? Drug use among vulnerable groups of young people', *Drugs: Education, Prevention and Policy*, No 5, pp. 213–16.

Moshowitz, J. M. (1989), 'The primary prevention of alcohol problems: a critical review of the research literature', *Journal of Studies on Alcohol*, No 50, pp. 54–88.

'Tackling drugs to build a better Britain' (1998), *The government's 10-year strategy for tackling drug misuse*, London, The Stationery Office.

UK Anti-drugs Coordinator (1999), *First annual report and national plan*, London, Central Office of Information.

Wragg, J. (1990), 'The longitudinal evaluation of a primary school drug education program: did it work?', *Drug Education Journal of Australia*, No 4, pp. 33–44.

Further reading

Advisory Council on the Misuse of Drugs (1988), *AIDS and drug misuse*. Part 1, London, HMSO.

Advisory Council on the Misuse of Drugs (1982), *Treatment and rehabilitation*, London, HMSO.

CHAPTER 4

EVALUATION AND DRUG-PREVENTION POLICY: THE GALICIAN PLAN ON DRUGS

Manuel Araujo Gallego

Advances in the development of images in the mind and advances in knowledge are measured much better by the history of questions than that of answers. Thus, in the final instance, a brain that thinks, thinks of the centre of the world alone. And though thought may not start with a question, it does end with an answer. For this reason, be more wary of answers. For answering represents a process of adaptation, while posing questions is an act of rebellion. (Jorge Wagensberg)

A brief description of Galicia

Galicia is one of the 17 autonomous communities of the Spanish State, located in the north-west of the Iberian peninsula. It covers an area of 29 575 km^2, bordering the Cantabrian Sea to the north, the Atlantic Ocean to the west, Portugal to the south and the autonomous communities of Asturias and Castilla-León to the east.

Galicia's population of over 2.7 million has a density of 93 inhabitants per km^2, higher than that of Spain as a whole (78 per km^2), but lower than that of the European Union (116 per km^2). 49 % of all the population centres in Spain are located in Galicia, although the region's inhabitants are distributed unequally, with a greater density on the coastal fringe than inland. The birth rate in Galicia is negative — minus 1.2 per 1 000 inhabitants, compared with 1.4 per 1 000 in Spain and 3.0 per 1 000 across the EU. Life expectancy at birth is 74.2 years for men and 81.5 for women, higher than life expectancy either in Spain or across the European Union.

21.7 % of Galicia's economically active population work in agriculture and fishing (compared to 8.6 % in Spain and 5.0 % across the EU), 27.8 % in industry (29.4 % in Spain and 29.8 % across the EU) and 50.4 % in the service sector (62.0 % in Spain and 65.1 % across the EU). From 1994 to 1996, gross domestic product per inhabitant was EUR 8 946, compared with EUR 11 278 in Spain and EUR 17 377 across the EU. Galicia has 17.3 % unemployment, compared with 18.8 % in Spain and 10.2 % in the EU ([27]).

([27]) 1998 data.

The importance of evaluation in Galicia

Evaluation is one of the guiding principles of the *Plan de Galicia sobre drogas 1997–2000* (Galician plan on drugs (GPD) — Consellería de Sanidade e Servicios Sociais, 2000a), approved by the government of Galicia on 23 January 1997 and by the parliament of Galicia on 27 June 1997. Research and evaluation of the plan itself are also governed by this strategic objective. Given the concept's status as a guiding principle, the requirement to undertake evaluation affects all the programmes carried out in the various areas of competence of the GPD — whether drug prevention, assistance to drug users, rehabilitation or training drug workers.

This mandate to evaluate has its origins in the *Lei de Galicia sobre drogas* [28] (Galician law on drugs (GLD) — Consellería de Sanidade e Servicios Sociais, 1996). This regulation covers many areas of drug demand reduction — from preventing drug consumption (including reducing the availability of alcohol and tobacco) to the budgetary commitments of public administrations to fund such activities — and states that evaluation systems are a compulsory minimum requirement of the plan on drugs. The GLD also refers explicitly to the concept in the articles that establish criteria for planning and managing demand-reduction activities in Galicia.

Reflecting the importance accorded to evaluation in Galicia, a drug monitoring centre, the Observatoria de Galicia sobre Drogas, was created in 1996 specifically to evaluate both the extent of the drug problem in the region and the initiatives introduced to combat it.

In line with the approach of the World Health Organisation, evaluation is understood here as a systematic means of acquiring empirical knowledge and using the lessons learned to change or improve a programme in order to facilitate more informed planning and decision-making.

Evaluation as a guide for allocating resources

Evaluation is not a new concept in Galicia, even though particular attention has only been focused on this task since 1994. In 1988, the first regional epidemiological study into drug use (EDIS, 1988) produced an epidemiological risk index or 'priority' index to help ensure the equitable distribution of resources for drug prevention within Galicia. Since then, four similar studies have been carried out, each with it own risk index (EDIS, 1992, 1994, 1996, 2000).

The three priority regions for drug prevention in Galicia include the following health areas:

- La Coruña, Santiago and Vigo (highest priority);
- El Ferrol, Lugo, Orense and Pontevedra (medium priority);
- Cervo, Monforte, O Barco and O Salnés (lowest priority).

---

(28) No 2/1996 of 8 May 1996.

These three regions have remained unchanged since the first report was produced in 1988 except for small internal variations, notably in the second region [29].

Table 1: Priority regions for drug prevention

Region	1988		1992		1994		1996		1998	
	PI	PO	PI	PO	PI	PO	PI	PO	PI	PO
Highest priority										
La Coruña	1.987	2	1.952	2	1.985	2	1.986	2	2.346	1
Santiago	1.556	3	1.752	3	1.723	3	1.723	3	2.067	3
Vigo	2.034	1	2.149	1	2.275	1	2.086	1	2.252	2
Medium priority										
El Ferrol	0.835	5	0.574	5	0.648	4	0.730	7	0.486	6
Lugo	0.392	7	0.558	6	0.645	5	0.740	6	0.740	5
Orense	0.395	6	0.356	7	0.588	6	0.941	4	0.941	4
Pontevedra	1.243	4	0.651	4	0.533	7	0.762	5	0.457	7
Lowest priority										
Cervo	0.027	9	0.057	9	0.138	9	0.110	9	0.083	9
Monforte	0.312	8	0.240	8	0.072	11	0.096	10	0.072	10
O Barco ([a])	—	—	—	—	0.076	10	0.061	11	0.030	11
O Salnés ([a])	—	—	—	—	0.168	8	0.216	8	0.120	8

NB:
PI = priority index or risk index.
PO = priority order of the regions according to the risk index.
([a]) The health regions of O Barco and O Salnés did not exist in 1988 and 1992.

Prioritising the areas where drug-prevention programmes are most needed allows the available resources to be distributed across Galicia based on an accurate assessment of needs.

Table 2 below compares the risk index from the 1998 study (EDIS, 2000) with the funding allocated to drug-prevention, assistance and social-rehabilitation programmes in the 11 health areas.

([29]) Prior to the 1994 report, the health areas of O Barco and O Salnés did not exist as such. The councils of which they are now constituted then formed part of Pontevedra and Monforte.

Table 2: Comparison of epidemiological priority and financial resources allocated

Epidemiological priority (a)	Health area	Financial resources allocated (b)		Financial priority
		EUR	% of total budget	
1	La Coruña	1 430 377	17.2	2
2	Vigo	1 949 812	23.5	1
3	Santiago	1 135 384	13.7	3
4	Orense	523 719	6.3	6
5	Lugo	523 150	6.3	7
6	El Ferrol	988 605	11.9	4
7	Pontevedra	740 232	8.9	5
8	O Salnés	455 321	5.5	8
9	Cervo	237 078	2.9	10
10	Monforte	251 454	3.0	9
11	O Barco	76 184	0.9	11

NB:
(a) Based on EDIS (2000).
(b) 1988 to 1999.

Evaluation systems

The Galician plan on drugs includes two specific evaluation systems: the Sistema de evaluación asistencial (Assistance evaluation system — SEA); and the Sistema de evaluación de programas de prevención e incorporación social (Prevention and social rehabilitation programmes evaluation system — SEPI).

The SEA has been operational since 1 January 1994 and provides information about drug users in treatment and the help they receive in the care system. The SEA analyses data at four levels from:

- the care system;
- each treatment programme within the care system as a whole;
- the individual treatment centres;
- each programme within each treatment centre.

Information on the various treatment programmes — especially drug-free, methadone-maintenance and naltrexone-maintenance programmes — is featured in the SEA manual (Consellería de Sanidade e Servicios Sociais, 1994). The SEA uses three indicators — time in treatment, reasons for leaving the programme and the activities undertaken — and the results of these indicators for each treatment centre are used to set the annual quantitative and qualitative objectives to be achieved by the centre and to allocate its budget.

Work on the second evaluation system, the SEPI, began in 1996 and its manual (Conselleria de Sanidade e Servicios Sociais, 2000b) and tools have now been finalised. The system was created to assess individual drug-prevention programmes, as well as the general objectives of the region's drug-prevention and rehabilitation policy as a whole. In this context, the SEPI was structured as an operational tool to help ensure coherence both within individual drug-prevention programmes and between the various related initiatives undertaken throughout Galicia.

The system's overall objectives are:

- to collect information on drug-prevention programmes and how the GPD is integrated into social structures;
- to facilitate the analysis and development of these programmes and the decision-making relating to them, as well as of procedures and planning in the drug-prevention field as a whole;
- to enable more complex types of evaluation to be carried out in the long term once the system of prioritising each area's drug-prevention needs has been fully established through regular information collection.

It should be emphasised that not only the individual programmes, but also the overall field of drug prevention itself is subject to evaluation. The field itself is seen in this context as a 'metaprogramme' encompassing the individual initiatives carried out by the voluntary associations and local councils that form part of the GPD network. As a result, when assessing the value and viability of individual programmes, it is not only their design that is analysed, but also how well their implementation, objectives and scope match the requirements and priorities set out in the plan on drugs.

The SEPI collects information at two crucial stages: when the programme is designed; and when the final reports and results are produced. A series of tools or protocols allows drug-prevention information to be gathered in a standardised fashion adapted to each specific setting, whether the community, the education system, the family, the workplace or youth settings.

Evaluating the individual programmes

The criteria for evaluating individual programmes are based on three factors. The first is the suitability of the programmes, which is assessed in relation to the priorities set out in the GPD.

The second factor is the clarity of the design, which examines the programme's characteristics and internal consistency at the outset, as well as analysing the relationship between the programme's underlying motive, objectives and activities. It seems obvious that a well-designed programme is more likely to tackle practical problems successfully and will allow the relation between the actions undertaken and the objectives achieved to be identified. The SEPI studies all programmes via a protocol known as the programme presentation document. This document provides a standard format in which the teams involved can present their programmes, and also serves as a reference guide during the planning process. The programme presentation document provides the following basic information:

- a justification of the chosen means of intervention by analysing the situation and the alternative options available;
- a description of the programme's characteristics and methodology;
- a description of the target population and context;
- a description of the programme's general and specific objectives;
- a description of the activities planned;
- a programme schedule;
- the human resources available;
- the material resources available;
- how the programme will be coordinated;
- the programme budget.

The third factor is the analysis of the programme's implementation once it has been carried out. This investigation examines the relationship between the initial objectives and the final outcomes to assess the extent to which the initial goals have been achieved. Such an analysis is necessary since, during the implementation of a programme, changes are often made to the original plan. A standard form has also been drawn up to facilitate this task.

Evaluating the metaprogramme

The data obtained at the individual programme level are then analysed to identify trends and developments in the drug-prevention field as a whole. The SEPI provides a set of indicators obtained from the data in the programme presentation forms and in the implementation report. From this information, collected both at the outset and on completion of the programme, a comparison can be drawn between forecasts and achievements.

Phases of the SEPI

The three main phases of the evaluation system are presented in Table 3.

Table 3: Phases of the SEPI

Phase	Objective	Tools	Outcome
1	annual analysis of drug-prevention programmes	— programme presentation document — evaluation plan for programme design and planning	analysis and evaluation of drug-prevention programmes
2	description of initial situation and procedure	— charts and calculation sheets	analysis and evaluation of initial situation
3	final annual evaluation of drug-prevention programmes and metaprogramme	— implementation reports for each programme — charts monitoring initial and final situation	evaluation of final situation

Indicators

The indicators used by the system can be grouped into four types:

- indicators of scope, which refer to the field targeted by each programme and activity in terms of location and population as well as of scale;
- indicators of activity, which describe the different actions according to the following categories:
  - awareness-raising and information;
  - training, including courses, seminars, conferences and discussion groups;
  - leisure and free time;
  - sport;
  - vocational workshops, for example on computing or gardening;
  - coordination meetings among drug professionals, organisations and associations and local authorities;
- personnel or performance indicators, which assess the abilities of the professionals and volunteers who implement the programmes;
- cost indicators, which examine the programme budget.

These indicators can also be classified according to the following programme criteria:

- all drug-prevention programmes (the equivalent of the metaprogramme level);
- the fields into which the programmes are grouped, such as community, school, family, youth;
- the classification given to the activities undertaken, as described above;
- geographical areas, whether health areas, provinces or Galicia as a whole.

Which of the available measures is most useful for planning and evaluating drug-prevention initiatives is not yet clear. Combining the indicator types (scope, activity, performance and cost) and the programme criteria (metaprogramme, fields, classification of activities and geographical area) could lead to a very high number of instruments which, in practice, would render the evaluation process completely inoperable. Instead, a limited number of indicators are needed offering a powerful enough tool to allow the tasks undertaken to be accurately assessed.

Tables 4 and 5 below present data from 1999 for some possible indicators.

Table 4 shows that:

- 38 % of all local councils in Galicia (119 out of 315) run drug-prevention and social-rehabilitation programmes;
- the potential target population of these programmes throughout Galicia is 68 %, although only 18 % actually take part in them;
- the cost per head of the metaprogramme for the user population is EUR 3.32, but is higher in the geographically smaller and less densely populated provinces, such as Lugo and Orense;
- the greater proliferation of these programmes in Pontevedra and La Coruña corresponds to the greater prevalence of drug use in these provinces.

Table 4: Drug-prevention and social-rehabilitation programmes by province and population

Province	Local councils		Programmes		Population		Cost per head (in EUR)	
	No (a)	% (b)	No	% (c)	potential clients (d)	clients (d)	potential clients	clients
La Coruña (e)	39	41	92	38	69	22	0.81	2.53
Lugo (f)	24	36	27	11	59	9	0.70	4.81
Orense (g)	30	33	28	12	59	12	0.77	3.74
Pontevedra (h)	26	42	95	39	74	20	0.75	2.82
All Galicia	119	38	242	100	68	18	0.89	3.32

NB:

(a) Number of local councils per province that run drug-prevention and social-rehabilitation programmes.

(b) Number of local councils per province that run drug-prevention and social-rehabilitation programmes as a percentage of all the local councils in that province.

(c) Number of drug-prevention and social-rehabilitation programmes per province as a percentage of the total number of such programmes in Galicia.

(d) (Potential) clients as a percentage of the total population.

(e) La Coruña includes the health areas of El Ferrol, La Coruña and Santiago.

(f) Lugo includes the health areas of Cervo, Lugo and Monforte.

(g) Orense includes the health areas of O Barco and Orense.

(h) Pontevedra includes the health areas of O Salnés, Pontevedra and Vigo.

Table 5 presents the geographical distribution of the 242 drug-prevention programmes by their field of action as percentages of the total number of drug-prevention programmes in each province.

The table shows that the greatest number of drug-prevention programmes in Galicia focus on information and training (21.5 %), schools (20.7 %), the family (19 %) and young people (17.3 %). Information and training initiatives include teacher training, school programmes cover all educational levels up to university, the family projects include educating parents and families, and youth initiatives are dominated by the 'Cinema and health' programme. The situation portrayed in Table 5 reflects the priorities laid down in the Galician plan on drugs which emphasises schools, the family and young people as targets for drug prevention.

Table 6 illustrates the regional distribution of school drug-prevention programmes which use specially designed teaching materials.

Drug-prevention programmes are implemented in 31 % of all public and private schools in Galicia. Out of the total number of participating schools, 88 % are in the public sector (representing 32 % of all public schools) and 12 % in the private sector (representing 23 % of all private schools). The programme reaches a total of 101 952 pupils — 23 % of all schoolchildren in Galicia — and 4 912 teachers — 14 % of the total teaching staff.

Table 5: Geographical distribution of drug-prevention programmes by field of action

Province	Field of action							
	school	family	community	youth	information and training	legal and social assistance	social rehabilitation	work
La Coruña	20.6	17.4	4.3	17.4	19.6	4.3	13.0	2.2
Lugo	22.2	18.5	0	18.5	25.9	3.7	11.1	0
Orense	21.4	21.4	0	17.8	21.4	3.6	14.3	0
Pontevedra	20.0	20.0	4.3	16.8	22.1	2.1	13.7	1.0
All Galicia	20.7	19.0	3.3	17.3	21.5	3.3	13.2	1.2

NB:
All figures are percentages of the total number of drug-prevention programmes in each province.

Table 6: Regional distribution of school drug-prevention programmes

Province	No of schools	No of drug-prevention programmes	% of schools that run drug-prevention programmes
La Coruña	786	202	26
Lugo	225	93	41
Orense	198	48	24
Pontevedra	681	234	34
All Galicia	1 890	577	31

NB:
Data are for the 1998 to 1999 school year.

Problems with evaluation systems

Problems and difficulties will always arise in the design and implementation of any evaluation system. These obstacles must be faced and resolved if that system is to succeed in promoting rational decision-making and in facilitating the planning of drug-prevention programmes. While a list of potential problems would be practically endless since new difficulties constantly appear, the following are among the most common obstacles encountered in evaluation:

- uncertainty surrounding the concept of drug prevention itself;
- the heterogeneity of the institutions taking part;
- the need for an inter-sectorial aspect to the evaluation;
- difficulties among the teams who provide information to the evaluation and to the planners and politicians who base their decisions on the evaluation results.

The GPD, the GLD and the framework document on prevention (Comisión asesora, 1993) all provide a fairly clearly defined notion of drug prevention, setting out the highest-priority fields and programmes. While this has reduced the level of uncertainty surrounding the concept of drug prevention, homogeneity cannot be fully assumed at the outset because the projects are only gradually adapted to the contents of these documents.

The heterogeneity of the institutions involved is linked to the existence of various voluntary associations and local councils, as well as to internal differences within each of these groups. To establish a single system of evaluation, common elements have to be identified. At the same time, however, it is crucial that the different approaches of the various bodies are taken into account, given that the GPD seeks to be an integrating force and that the problem of drug addiction demands action from many different angles. This heterogeneity does not affect the evaluation of programme designs, which must fulfil certain common criteria, but it does affect other types of assessment relating to the programme's requirements, justification and results.

Integrating all sectors of the community and all agencies active within it — one of the goals of the GPD — is a complex task since it presupposes the involvement of a wide range of social agencies, government departments and other bodies. In such a context, consensus becomes an essential requirement for planning in order to ensure that the different views are taken into account and the various resources available brought into play. Thus, evaluation must consider the programme's potential for achieving this multi-sectorial integration.

Systematic evaluation processes inevitably interfere with the normal working practices of the teams involved, and inappropriate intervention risks creating excessive levels of bureaucracy, diverting the attention of the professionals from actually implementing the drug-prevention programme. Thus, it is vital that evaluation systems are instituted with care and that the teams involved understand their purpose and utility, as well as the benefits they can gain from the methods used and the results obtained.

Providing new tools and systems with which the teams have to work, obtaining information, inputting data into databases and analysing them all take up time and disrupt working patterns. New capacities often have to be introduced to deal with these additional tasks and extra elements have to be juggled, including decisions relating to the treatment and analysis of data. Introducing new working practices means incorporating new routines, and that alone requires some effort. In addition, the optimal performance of these systems is evident only after they have been operational for several years.

Conclusions

It is vital that the professional teams that undertake evaluations understand fully what it is hoped the process will achieve, and this is particularly true during implementation. Neither false expectations nor misunderstandings should be created. Evaluation is not a magic solution; it is simply a means of making the decision-making process more rational and a tool for increasing knowledge about a phenomenon — in this case drug use — and how to influence it.

A large proportion of what has been said in relation to 'frontline' professional teams also applies to planners and politicians, especially concerning evaluation as a 'magic solution'. Just as some professionals think that poor evaluation results may lead to the loss of their jobs, certain planners and politicians may be tempted to use those same results as an excuse for reducing the budgets of less productive programmes.

Clearly if a programme is not working satisfactorily — that is, if it is incapable of meeting its objectives — there is no sense in it continuing and using human or material resources. However, a decision to cancel a programme can only be taken after detailed examination of why it is not achieving its objectives. In other words, for drug-prevention professionals, evaluation is the best way of improving the effectiveness and efficiency of programmes and not an acceptable excuse for reducing budgets. The evaluation process, and the technology at its disposal, however, also have their limitations. For this reason, evaluation processes must be applied with modesty and honesty, but also with firmness.

References

Comisión asesora para el desarrollo del programa de prevención del consumo de drogas (1993), *Prevención en drogodependencias. Documento-marco,* Colección Drogodependencias 10, Santiago de Compostela, Consellería de Sanidade, Xunta de Galicia.

Consellería de Sanidade e Servicios Sociais (2000a), *Plan de Galicia sobre drogas 1997–2000,* Colección Drogodependencias 22, second edition, Santiago de Compostela, Consellería de Sanidade, Xunta de Galicia.

Consellería de Sanidade e Servicios Sociais (2000b), *Manual del Sistema para la evaluación de los programas de prevención e incorporación social,* Santiago de Compostela, Consellería de Sanidade, Xunta de Galicia.

Consellería de Sanidade e Servicios Sociais (1996), *Lei de Galicia sobre drogas,* Colección Drogodependencias 20, Santiago de Compostela, Consellería de Sanidade, Xunta de Galicia.

Consellería de Sanidade e Servicios Sociais (1994), *Sistema de evaluación asistencial (SEA),* Santiago de Compostela, Consellería de Sanidade, Xunta de Galicia.

Equipo de Investigación Sociológica (EDIS) (2000), *O consumo de drogas en Galicia V,* Colección Drogodependencias 23, Santiago de Compostela, Consellería de Sanidade, Xunta de Galicia.

EDIS (1996), *O consumo de drogas en Galicia IV,* Colección Drogodependencias 21, Santiago de Compostela, Consellería de Sanidade, Xunta de Galicia.

EDIS (1994), *O consumo de drogas en Galicia III,* Colección Drogodependencias 18, Santiago de Compostela, Consellería de Sanidade, Xunta de Galicia.

EDIS (1992), *O consumo de drogas en Galicia II*, Colección Drogodependencias 11, Santiago de Compostela, Consellería de Sanidade, Xunta de Galicia.

EDIS (1988), *O consumo de drogas en Galicia I*, Colección Drogodependencias 1, Santiago de Compostela, Consellería de Sanidade, Xunta de Galicia

Further reading

Amigo Quintana, M., et al. (1995), *Materiais Didácticos para a prevención do consumo de drogas, Programa de Educación para a Saúde na Escola*, Santiago de Compostela, Consellería de Sanidade e Servicios Sociais, Xunta de Galicia, and Consellería de Educación e Ordenación Universitaria.

Wagensberg, J. (1994), *Ideas sobre la complejidad del mundo. Colección metatemas*, Barcelona, Tusquets editores.

Improving drug-prevention practice

Part II

Introduction

In Chapter 5, Christoph Kröger examines how the EMCDDA's Guidelines for the evaluation of drug prevention *have been both distributed and implemented at European level. He describes the quantitative (number of guidelines distributed per country) and qualitative (interviews with users) methods used to evaluate the manual's impact, and the settings in which the guidelines have been most commonly applied.*

Gregor Burkhart continues this theme in Chapter 6, explaining how different EU Member States have adapted the guidelines to their national contexts and highlighting two case studies, one from France and one from Italy. He then describes other EMCDDA initiatives to promote the evaluation of drug prevention, including the Exchange on drug demand-reduction action (EDDRA) information system and the Evaluation instruments bank. The author concludes by identifying how such tools could be further developed to better serve the needs of European drug-prevention professionals.

In Chapter 7, Krzysztof Ostaszewski and his colleagues demonstrate how a US primary-prevention programme aimed at reducing drinking among schoolchildren was modified for use in Polish schools. The authors explain how the US material was adapted to a different cultural context, and describe the initial pilot study as well as the design, procedure and results of an outcome evaluation of the programme. The chapter concludes with the lessons learned from this innovative experience.

Amador Calafat examines drug-prevention initiatives targeted specifically at recreational drug users in Chapter 8. He identifies the characteristics and significance of this relatively new phenomenon and describes the forms of prevention that have grown up in Europe in response to it. The author then suggests concrete ways of raising awareness of the specific problems associated with recreational drug use and of improving both preventive interventions themselves and their evaluation.

CHAPTER 5

IMPLEMENTING THE EMCDDA *GUIDELINES FOR THE EVALUATION OF DRUG PREVENTION*

Christoph Kröger

In 1996, the European Monitoring Centre for Drugs and Drug Addiction (EMCDDA) began to promote the evaluation of drug-prevention interventions. One of the Centre's strategies to demonstrate the importance of such assessments was to develop, test and distribute guidelines for the evaluation of drug prevention.

The guidelines were drafted by the German national focal point of the Reitox network, the Institut für Therapieforschung (IFT), Munich, with the assistance of drug-prevention and evaluation experts from other European Member States and from the National Institute on Drug Abuse (NIDA) in the United States. A draft version of the guidelines was tested in a feasibility phase in 1997 with the participation of 20 projects from 13 EU countries. The final version of the guidelines was then translated into all 11 official EU languages and distributed as a working document in both paper and electronic format. In autumn 1998, the *Guidelines for the evaluation of drug prevention* were published in English (EMCDDA, 1998).

The EMCDDA contracted the Centro de Estudios sobre la Promoción de la Salud (CEPS), Madrid, and the IFT to monitor and evaluate the distribution and implementation of the guidelines from August 1998 to May 1999 and to obtain feedback from recipients about how they were planning to use the manual. The national focal points of the Reitox network and other national partner organisations were asked to distribute the guidelines free of charge and to record to whom they were sent. A flyer providing information on the manual's aim and content and an order form were produced to be distributed as and when it was deemed appropriate. A feedback sheet was also developed and attached to the guidelines which the recipients were asked to complete and return to a national address.

Almost 1 200 copies of the guidelines were distributed by the EMCDDA, its national partners, CEPS and the IFT between April and December 1998 (see Table 1 below).

Table 1 shows that a maximum of 263 and a minimum of two copies were distributed per country. These figures should, however, be interpreted with caution since they are unlikely to reflect the actual numbers of copies circulated in a specific country, but only those recorded by the national partners. Paper and electronic copies may well have been made and distributed without the knowledge of the

Table 1: Number of copies of the guidelines distributed, April to December 1998

Country	No of copies
Belgium	84
Denmark	263
Germany	173
Greece	38
Spain	132
France	22
Ireland	32
Italy	51
Luxembourg	8
Netherlands	9
Austria	41
Portugal	86
Finland	32
Sweden	2
United Kingdom	205
Non-EU	7
Total	1 185

national partners. It should also be borne in mind that some institutions were unable to document their dissemination very accurately because of a high workload and/or other priorities.

During the nine-month period, almost 500 completed feedback sheets were received. Table 2 below shows that most recipients intended to use the guidelines for drug-prevention work in schools and the community.

The feedback sheets did not, however, give information on how the recipients actually used the guidelines. Instead, telephone interviews were conducted with a randomly selected sample of 25 of the 69 German recipients who returned the feedback sheet. All recipients had received the guidelines about 12 months prior to the interview. The semi-structured interview included the following questions:

- Did you receive the guidelines?
- Did you read the guidelines?
- Did you apply the guidelines?

The sample was also asked for detailed (qualitative) feedback and to rate different aspects of the guidelines.

Figure 1 below shows the main results of the interviews. Three of those interviewed (12 %) did not remember the guidelines, although a feedback sheet with their names had been received. Six interviewees (24 %) remembered ordering and receiving the guidelines, but had not yet read them. The majority of the recipients (64 %) said that they had read at least parts of the guidelines and about 28 % had also used the guidelines in their work.

Table 2: Drug-prevention field in which the guidelines were intended for use

Drug-prevention field	No of respondents	% of respondents
School programme	112	23.1
Community programme	102	21.1
Recreational youth setting	67	13.8
Early-childhood intervention	55	11.4
Mass-media campaign	42	8.7
Outreach work	31	6.4
Telephone help-line	16	3.3
Other	59	12.2
Total	484	100.0

These figures may appear disappointing at first glance, but could have been expected given that the copies of the guidelines were given away for free. This may well have encouraged people to order them without really intending to use them.

Extrapolating cautiously from these figures, it can be assumed that about 600 people in the EU Member States were not only interested in, but also read, the guidelines, and this should be seen as an encouraging first result. The readiness of the target group to apply the guidelines in planning drug-prevention evaluations appears to be at an intermediate phase. Using a model of eight stages of readiness, this phase can be characterised as 'pre-planning' or 'preparation'. The eight stages of readiness are:

- no awareness;
- denial;
- vague awareness;
- pre-planning;
- preparation;
- initiation;
- standardisation;
- professionalisation.

Drug-prevention practitioners in Europe clearly have more than just a vague awareness of the guidelines and the need for evaluation measures in their field. While they appear interested and motivated to engage in evaluation, they are not yet at the stages of standardisation or professionalisation.

Conclusions

Implementation of the *Guidelines for the evaluation of drug prevention* is a long-term process that is still at an early stage, but first results should encourage their further distribution. This future dissemination relies, however, on personal and institutional engagement which in turn depends on how important this task is considered as well, inevitably, as the resources available. Both the motivation of the institutions respon-

Figure 1: Results of telephone interviews with 25 German recipients of the guidelines

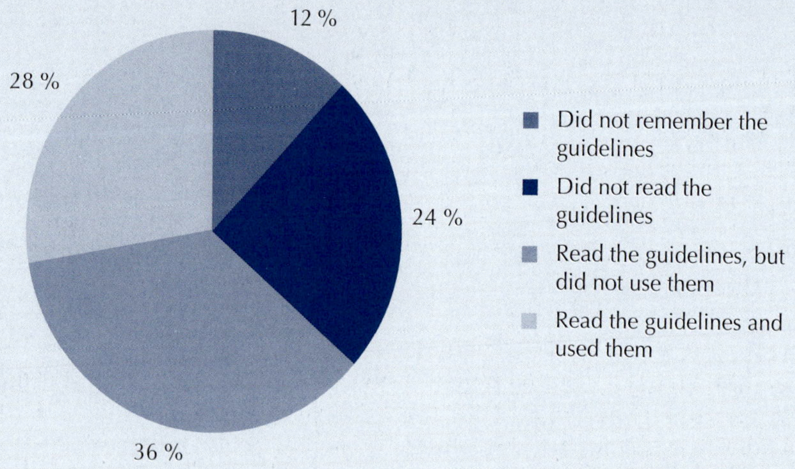

sible for the distribution (in the first instance the Reitox national focal points) and their capacity to undertake this task need to be enhanced. This could be achieved by identifying national 'key persons' and encouraging them to distribute the guidelines. More active advertising in newsletters or at conferences is also necessary.

While the *Guidelines for the evaluation of drug prevention* clearly cannot, and should not, substitute personal communication and training, they do already play an important role in promoting both the concept and practice of evaluation in the drug-prevention field.

References

European Monitoring Centre for Drugs and Drug Addiction (1998), *Guidelines for the evaluation of drug prevention*, Manuals No 1, Lisbon, EMCDDA.

CHAPTER 6

EMCDDA TOOLS FOR EVALUATING DRUG PREVENTION

Gregor Burkhart

The first tool developed by the European Monitoring Centre for Drugs and Drug Addiction (EMCDDA) to promote the evaluation of drug prevention was the *Guidelines for the evaluation of drug prevention* (EMCDDA, 1998). In monitoring and evaluating how the guidelines were received by drug-prevention professionals in Europe [30], the EMCDDA obtained valuable information about the manual's utility, together with indications of areas for further development and new issues to be addressed.

In a second phase, some EU Member States have gone further than simply distributing the guidelines and collecting feedback, and have adapted them to their specific national contexts. These national interpretations have both broadened the original scope of the manual and provided further inspiration for improving evaluation practice. Two examples of national adaptations, one from France and one from Italy, are described below and demonstrate the types of initiative currently under way in the EU to develop new tools to support the evaluation of drug prevention.

France

The French adaptation of the EMCDDA guidelines added information about the organisational and management aspects of evaluation to ensure that all available background information would be accessible to drug-prevention project managers in France. This initiative reflects the growing evaluation culture in France which is a priority of the Mission interministérielle de lutte contre la drogue et la toxicomanie (MILDT, 1999).

Among the innovative aspects of the French version of the manual is the emphasis it places on project management and decision-making. In this context, project management includes:

- forecasting;
- monitoring the implementation of the programme and assessing the relevance of its individual components;

[30] This process is described in detail in Chapter 5.

- adapting the project design to new developments and integrating new elements as required.

Decision-making involves:

- endorsing and justifying activities;
- reusing a successful approach in other settings;
- allocating budgets.

The French version of the guidelines asks key questions such as:

- Why undertake the evaluation?
- Who is the evaluation for?
- How should it be managed?
- What can be evaluated?

The practical evaluation questions, however, are very close to those in the original EMCDDA version, although illustrative examples are taken from a French evaluation study (Choquet and Lagadic, 1997).

Italy

In Italy, a working group of experts from Ancona, Bergamo, Ferrara, Modena, Rome, Turin and Urbino has adapted the guidelines to the specific needs of Italian drug-prevention practice. The EMCDDA version was considered too focused on drug abuse as the object of prevention programmes whereas most Italian initiatives were more concerned with social interaction, well-being and more general aspects of health promotion.

This view illustrates a persistent misconception regarding the EMCDDA's guidelines which, as a universal pan-European tool, intentionally do not refer to the specific concepts, theories, strategies or intermediate objectives found in the literature which could be used to tackle the problem of drug abuse. Instead, the manual aims to be neither context- nor culture-specific.

Identifying the most suitable theoretical and strategic framework for a drug-prevention programme in whatever country or region is the task of the programme leader. There is an apparent need among practitioners for more explicit statements and support in formulating the intermediate objectives (such as enhancing social competence and life skills) and final goals (preventing drug use or abuse) of specific programmes. While the EMCDDA's evaluation guidelines leave this task to the programme leaders, the Italian version includes explicit advice for formulating programme objectives. In referring to a concrete set of theories and strategies, the Italian adaptation is more explanatory than the EMCDDA original, albeit also more limited in scope.

The Italian guidelines include flow-chart-like sequences of questions for several topics, for example:

objectives? → indicators? → how? (instruments) → when? (planning) → who? (actors and target group)

These questions are based on those used to collect national data on drug demand-reduction programmes for inclusion in the EMCDDA's Exchange on drug demand-reduction action (EDDRA) information system, and the logical sequence of these questions underlines the importance of internal coherence in evaluation and programme description ([31]). These questions could be further developed to create an interactive electronic tool that would ask relevant questions for evaluation in the right sequence depending on the specific context and stage of a particular programme. Such an electronic tool could also integrate the EDDRA questionnaire — which would both adapt it more effectively to the working practices of the programme teams and facilitate its completion — as well as basic definitions of evaluation concepts.

Another interesting feature of the Italian adaptation is the use of socio-demographic mapping to show changes in relationships between groups and neighbourhoods. This information can facilitate the more effective allocation of resources, needs assessment and evaluation.

COST A-6: Evaluation of action against drug abuse in Europe

The publication *Evaluation research in regard to primary prevention of drug abuse* (Springer and Uhl, 1998) of the Evaluation of action against drug abuse in Europe (COST A-6) working group reiterates the need for a clear definition of evaluation concepts. In the words of Springer and Uhl, 'everything nowadays is evaluation'. The EMCDDA guidelines, however, are based on a more 'common-sense' than scientific understanding of the concept of evaluation, and it may now be necessary to redress this by classifying the types of evaluation referred to according to the more scientific COST A-6 definition. The work of this group has also highlighted the need to include ethical considerations on evaluation in future versions of the EMCDDA guidelines.

Evaluation and EDDRA training

To distribute the EMCDDA guidelines and to expect drug-prevention practitioners to use them is, however, insufficient. Programme leaders need training in applying even minimal evaluation standards in order to accept that evaluations do not have to be carried out at expert level. Above all, practitioners need to be able to see the concrete benefits of evaluation. These benefits include being part of a network of information exchange and making their programmes publicly accessible via systems such as EDDRA, thus gaining greater visibility for their work.

([31]) The EDDRA information system is discussed in greater detail in Chapters 11 and 12.

As a result, the EMCDDA is jointly organising with the Reitox national focal points training seminars in the EU Member States. These seminars are designed to promote evaluation practice among both professionals and regional decision-makers, and to enhance the skills necessary for working with the EDDRA system and for completing the EDDRA questionnaire. These workshops will also be a valuable source of feedback and suggestions from the field and will further strengthen the link between the EMCDDA and demand-reduction practice at EU level.

Evaluation instruments bank

The *Guidelines for the evaluation of drug prevention* and the EDDRA information system are not the only EMCDDA tools devised to promote evaluation. The Evaluation instruments bank (EIB) is a database of tools for assessing both drug-prevention and treatment initiatives ([32]). All the instruments for evaluating drug-prevention programmes contained in the bank are freely downloadable. Some of the tools for evaluating treatment, however, are protected by copyright and, while they cannot be freely downloaded, are all fully indexed and described with clear indications of where they can be obtained.

The bank contains over 150 prevention and treatment evaluation instruments together with three search mechanisms allowing for the rapid identification of the most suitable tools for the user's needs. The tools are presented according to the structure of the EMCDDA's evaluation guidelines, with a selection of instruments provided for each phase of a drug-prevention programme from planning to summative evaluation. The instruments included are those that have been found to be of most value and are most frequently cited in drug-prevention literature. The criteria used in the selection were:

- evidence of reliability and validity;
- ease of understanding;
- adaptability;
- grounding in current practice.

In creating the EIB, over 1 600 scientific and grey-literature publications were reviewed, more than 200 experts and practitioners responsible for developing treatment-evaluation tools were contacted, while the prevention instruments included in the bank and the rationale for their selection were analysed by a group of 12 experts from across the EU. Over 250 treatment-evaluation tools were reviewed and their scientific quality evaluated, and around 100 have been included in the bank. Information is provided on the content, utility, scientific quality, accessibility, copyright, cost and source of each tool. All the treatment instruments accessible in the EIB are original, and their references have been published in the scientific literature. The bank includes summaries of more than 900 studies with links to specific instruments, and full bibliographies and references are available for all the tools and studies included.

([32]) The EIB will be available on-line via the EMCDDA website during 2000.

As a next step, the EMCDDA will add a mailing list for a direct-discussion forum of interested professionals to encourage feedback and proposals for the inclusion of more instruments or for their translation into other European languages. While the EIB currently only contains instruments in English, the database was designed to allow tools to be uploaded and accessed in several different languages. The EMCDDA would welcome any translations of current or new instruments in languages other than English.

Conclusions

The EMCDDA's existing tools for promoting the evaluation of drug prevention could be further developed in several ways.

Based on the Italian flow-chart idea, an integrated electronic version of the *Guidelines for the evaluation of drug prevention* could be developed with additional interactive features. This version would take the form of a computer programme that would ask relevant questions for evaluation in the right sequence according to the specific needs of an individual project. Such a tool could also include the EDDRA questionnaire and basic definitions of common concepts in evaluation, plus the EMCDDA's forthcoming guidelines for the evaluation of outreach work (33). Integrating these elements into a single interactive instrument would enable practitioners to identify more effectively those aspects of evaluation relevant to their specific situation.

Another significant contribution the EMCDDA could make in this area would be to use its central position in the Reitox network to create a pool of evaluation experiences, ideas, methods and theories. Information on the most common European approaches and strategies for drug prevention already held by the EMCDDA — in large part through the EDDRA system — could then be channelled back to European demand-reduction professionals.

References

Choquet, M., Lagadic, C. (1997), *Evaluation en milieu scolaire d'un programme de prévention primaire en matière de toxicomanie*, Villejuif, Inserm.

European Monitoring Centre for Drugs and Drug Addiction (1998), *Guidelines for the evaluation of drug prevention*, Manuals No 1, Lisbon, EMCDDA.

Mission interministérielle de lutte contre la drogue et la toxicomanie (1999), 'Plan triennal de lutte contre la drogue et de prévention des dépendances. 1999 — 2000 — 2001'.

Springer, A., and Uhl, A. (Eds) (1998), *Evaluation research in regard to primary prevention of drug abuse*, Brussels, European Commission.

(33) The EMCDDA's guidelines for the evaluation of outreach work will be available in 2001.

CHAPTER 7

EVALUATING INNOVATIVE DRUG-PREVENTION PROGRAMMES: LESSONS LEARNED

Krzysztof Ostaszewski, Krzysztof Bobrowski, Anna Borucka, Katarzyna Okulicz-Kozaryn, Agnieszka Pisarska

Research has demonstrated that involving parents and peer leaders in drug-prevention initiatives targeted at young people may be a valuable approach since both parental and peer behaviour have been shown to influence the health-related choices made by adolescents. Parental involvement in drug-prevention initiatives may improve parent–child communication about substance use (Williams et al., 1995a; Toomey et al., 1997; Williams and Perry, 1998; Williams et al., 1999), and may also influence young people's choice of non-drug-using friends (Rohrbach et al., 1995). Similarly, it has been shown that involving peer leaders in drug-prevention initiatives may improve their effectiveness (Schaps et al., 1981; Tobler, 1986; Klepp et al., 1986; Perry et al., 1989; Botvin et al., 1990; Komro et al., 1994; Perry et al., 1996).

In Poland, a number of new drug-prevention initiatives involving parents or peer leaders have been implemented over the past decade. However, low parental participation and logistical problems with using peer leaders, such as the extra burden this adds to their school timetable, can be serious obstacles. In this context, a two-year research project was launched by the Institute of Psychiatry and Neurology in Warsaw to adapt and evaluate an innovative US primary-prevention programme for fifth-grade schoolchildren, involving both parents and peer leaders, with a view to replicating it in Polish schools as a component of local-community drug-prevention action. The US programme, the Slick Tracy Home Team Program, was developed and evaluated by a team from the University of Minnesota as part of Project Northland (Perry et al., 1993; Williams et al., 1995a; Perry at al., 1996). The project was recommended to the Institute of Psychiatry and Neurology by the US National Institute on Alcohol Abuse and Alcoholism.

The Slick Tracy Home Team Program aims to prevent under-age drinking and consists of five teacher- and peer-led sessions combined with parent–child activities to be undertaken at home. Four booklets, one to be worked through each week, provide information on under-age drinking, alcohol advertising and modelling, peer pressure and the consequences of alcohol consumption. The activities in the booklets are designed to facilitate parent–child communication about alcohol and other substance use and to establish effective family rules to deal with under-age drinking. Elected peer leaders, trained by their teachers, introduce each booklet to their classmates and encourage them to participate in the activities with their parents. Pupils receive small incentives, such as sweets or pens, to encourage their active participation. At the end of the programme, a family evening is organised at which pupils present posters to their parents. The entire programme requires about 10 weeks to complete.

The Polish version of the US programme, Program Domowych Detektywów (Ostaszewski et al., 1998), is the result of:

- adapting the US teaching material to the Polish context;
- a pilot study focusing on cross-cultural adaptation of the programme;
- an outcome evaluation.

Evaluation of the programme consisted of a pilot study held in the 1997/98 school year, and an outcome study held in 1998 to 1999. Routine implementation of the programme began in the 1999/2000 school year and included producing materials, promoting the initiative and teacher training. The project followed to some extent the six-phase model of the process leading to the implementation of drug-prevention programmes (Uhl, 1998). These six phases are:

- basic research;
- prevention research;
- concept;
- development;
- testing;
- routine implementation.

Pilot study, 1997 to 1998

The pilot study (n = 90) used a combination of qualitative and quantitative methods, including observing classroom activities, analysing programme documentation, focus-group interviews with teachers, telephone interviews with randomly selected parents and pre- and post-test self-report questionnaires for students. The results of the pilot study showed that the programme functioned well in Polish schools (Ostaszewski et al., 1998). This is borne out by the positive opinions expressed by all groups involved in the programme — teachers, students and parents — and by direct observations.

Essential aspects of the pilot study were:

- high rates of parental participation in the programme (about 80 % of parents took part in one or more activities);
- high quality of the programme delivery (including adequate peer-leader involvement) which resulted in good student engagement in the programme;
- positive feedback from teachers;
- positive feedback from both pupils and parents concerning the programme as a whole as well as its individual elements.

However, the evaluation also identified two problem areas: the poor participation of children at risk of low academic achievement; and some limitations in teacher–parent cooperation. Of the six students (7 %) who did not participate in the home activities, all experienced problems at school. According to the teachers, the low participation of these pupils was associated with alcohol-related problems in their families. It is estimated that in Poland between 2 and 4 % of children live with an alcohol-dependent parent and an additional 14 % of children have at least one parent who regularly abuses alcohol (Sierosławski, 1997). The pilot study helped identify that during the programme some children at risk would need special attention or individual care from their teachers.

The second problem concerned teacher–parent cooperation. It was quite a new experience for teachers to share responsibility for delivering the programme with parents and, as a result, the teachers questioned whether the parents actually undertook the booklet activities with their children and if they really read the materials designed for them. The teachers felt that they should have greater control over what their pupils were taught during the programme. This opinion reflects a more general problem in the Polish school system — the low level of cooperation between schools and parents and the lack of partnership between them. As a result of the pilot study, the following modifications were made to improve teacher–parent cooperation:

- a leaflet was produced aimed specifically at parents;
- new content was added to the teacher manual to explain in more detail the specific roles of parents, teachers and peer leaders in the programme;
- several new presentations were included to stimulate parental participation in the family evening;
- it was recommended that teachers obtain parental consent before the start of the programme.

Teacher training was adapted to give precise advice on how to work with pupils whose parents did not participate in the booklet activities.

Outcome evaluation, 1998 to 1999

Design and subjects

The second phase of the evaluation focused on immediate outcomes and adopted a quasi-experimental design. The quality of the programme delivery was also controlled. The study sample (n = 440) consisted of fifth-grade pupils in 10 primary schools from Mokotów, a district of Warsaw. The school authorities agreed to participate in the programme and accepted random assignment to either the intervention or reference group. Five schools were assigned to the intervention group (n = 231) and five to the reference group (n = 209), which took part in the programme the following term.

The outcome evaluation was based on a self-report questionnaire. Pupils were assessed in their classrooms by trained staff at pre-test (September 1998) and at post-test (December 1998). Of the students monitored at post-test, 11 % dropped out leaving 393 (89 % of the original sample), and there were no differences in attrition rates between the intervention and reference groups. Eleven students (five from the intervention and six from the reference groups) were removed from the analysis because of inconsistent responses to at least three different questions. Thus the final study sample in the outcome analysis consisted of 382 students — 203 in the intervention and 179 in the reference group — or 87 % of the original study sample. There were no baseline differences between the groups in terms of the age of the pupils (the average age in both groups was 11.5 years at pre-test) or their family composition (86 % in the intervention group and 85 % in the reference group lived with two parents). Although the gender composition differed between the groups (54 % of the intervention group were boys compared to 48 % in the reference group), this variation did not reach statistical significance.

Scales of measurement

The main variables of interest were:

- alcohol use;
- intention to use alcohol;
- peer norms;
- parent-child communication about the consequences of drinking and smoking;
- perceived resistance skills;
- alcohol-related knowledge.

Of the six scales used to measure these variables, four (alcohol use, intention to drink, peer norms and resistance skills) met the statistical criteria for sufficient reliability and validity (Ostaszewski et al., 1999). The scale concerning parent-child communication demonstrated high internal consistency (alpha — 0.79), but some limited support for the construct validity. Although the alcohol-related knowledge scale did not perform well, either in reliability or construct-validity analyses, it was not excluded as there was no better multiple construct to measure the relevant knowledge. Scales were scored by adding the points for each individual item, with equal weights given to them.

Table 1 shows the characteristic of the six scales, examples of the individual items, and the internal coefficients and main source for each scale. Frequency of cigarette smoking and demographic variables were measured by single items.

Procedure

The Program Domowych Detektywów was implemented in the five intervention schools as part of the curriculum between October and December 1998. Teachers and school coordinators were given relevant materials and trained by programme staff in two four-hour sessions, and parental consent to the use of the programme in each school was obtained before the programme began. Peer leaders were elected by their classmates and trained by their teachers, and 'rewards' were given to participating pupils on completion of the first two booklets. The family evening parties

Table 1: Characteristics of the six scales used in the study

Scale	Items or examples of items	Alpha coefficient	Main source of the scale or items
Alcohol use (four items) ([a])	Q: 'How often have you drunk alcohol: in your lifetime, in the last year, in the last month, in the last week?' A: 'never', 'once', 'twice', 'three or more times'	0.74	Adapted from Johnston et al. (1993), Williams et al. (1995b)
Intention to use alcohol (three items)	Q: 'How likely is it that you will drink alcohol: in your lifetime, in the next year, in the next month?' A: five, ranging from 'I would not drink' to 'I would drink'	0.70	Adapted from Johnston et al. (1993), Williams et al. (1995b)
Peer norms (six items)	Q: 'Does your best friend drink alcohol?' A: 'yes', 'no' Q: 'How many of your friends smoked cigarettes last month?' A: four, ranging from 'none' to 'more than half'	0.63	Adapted from Williams et al. (1995b)
Parent-child communication (three items)	Q: 'Do your parents talk to you about the problems drinking alcohol can cause young people?' A: 'yes', 'no'	0.79	Adapted from Williams et al. (1995a)
Perceived resistance skills (five items)	Q: 'How sure are you that could say "no" if you were offered alcohol in the following situations: at a friend's house?...' A: five, ranging from 'I could say "no"' to 'I could not say "no"'	0.74	Adapted from Williams et al. (1995b)
Alcohol-related knowledge (five items)	Q: 'Alcohol gives people energy', 'Beer, alcohol and wine advertisements try to get people my age to think it's cool to drink' A: 'yes', 'no', 'don't know'	0.40	Adapted from Williams et al. (1995a)

NB:
([a]) Alcohol use = more than one sip of beer, wine, vodka or champagne.

were organised by teachers and school coordinators and parents were also actively involved in three schools. Each student who completed a presentation received a special diploma, and sweets, cakes and refreshments were also available. Teachers and school coordinators received a small amount of funding towards the cost of the evening from Warsaw school authorities.

Results of the process evaluation

The process evaluation was based on a combination of qualitative and quantitative methods:

- post-test questionnaires for students (n = 226) and parents (n = 158);
- two group interviews with teachers (n = 10);
- analyses of programme documentation.

The evaluation found that the programme had been fully implemented in all intervention schools. According to self-report data from both students and parents, over 90 % of the students participated in the booklet activities, most frequently with their mothers. Similar rates were identified from the teachers' classroom records. Girls, pupils in two-parent families and 'good' students were significantly more likely to complete more booklets. The rate of participation in the family evening was also high, with 74 % of students attending, 56 % with at least one parent.

Teachers were given two alternative methods of selecting peer leaders in the classroom: election from a whole group of students; or election from small, pre-selected groups. Although most of the choices were based on student popularity, group interviews with teachers established that the procedure differed from class to class. Some teachers modified the recommended method in different ways, while others tried to influence the selection. In a few classes, the election caused some competition between candidates, but according to the teachers this was only a marginal problem. Furthermore, there were no significant differences in satisfaction rates between peer leaders and participating students, which suggested that peer leaders were accepted in their new roles. In addition, being a leader was perceived by students as an honour. In the teachers' opinions, the trained peer leaders were very motivated and fully engaged in the programme activities. Although they experienced some difficulties with discipline in activities with small groups, they generally performed their tasks well or very well.

The process evaluation also identified some significant differences in the quality of the programme delivery. Students from three classes reported significantly lower rates of participation in the activities and much lower rates of satisfaction (see Table 2). Analyses of documentation and interviews with teachers confirmed that in these three classes there had been some defects in the programme implementation — such as shortening the classroom activities and poor preparation of the family evening — as well as inadequate cooperation between the school staff involved in the programme, insufficient parental acceptance of the programme and lack of commitment by the school authority. In this context, it was concluded that quality of programme delivery might be an important aspect of routine implementation.

Results of the outcome evaluation

Pre-test equivalence

There were no significant baseline differences between the intervention and reference groups in all alcohol-use and smoking items (see Table 3). A high percentage

Table 2: Programme participation and satisfaction rates in the intervention group

	Seven classes (n = 172)	Three classes (n = 59)	Chi-square	p
% participation in three or four booklets ([a])	94	64	33.5	p< 0.001
% participation in the family evening (student plus parents) ([b])	65	24	24.6	p< 0.001
% of highly or very highly satisfied students ([b])	75	37	23.6	p< 0.001

NB:
([a]) Identified from teachers' classroom records.
([b]) Identified from students' self-report questionnaires.
p = level of significance.

of 11-year-olds reporting alcohol use in their lifetime and the previous year was probably caused by including champagne in the list of alcoholic beverages. Some children may, for example, have reported alcohol use after having more than a sip of their parents' champagne during a New Year's Eve party. There were no significant discrepancies at pre-test in other outcome variables. Only one difference was identified — parents of pupils in the intervention group used alcohol more frequently at home: $p < 0.05$. This variable — besides gender — was controlled in the outcome analyses.

Outcomes

Analyses of the differences between the intervention and reference groups were tested using multiple analysis of variance (Manova) with an individual subject as the unit of analysis. In the first step, differences in alcohol use were analysed and in the second step the other five scales were analysed together. Comparison of the varia-

Table 3: Alcohol and cigarette use in the intervention and reference groups at pre-test

	% Intervention group (n = 203)	% Reference group (n = 179)	Chi-square	p
Alcohol use ([a])				
Lifetime	68.1	61.3	1.79	n.s.
Last year	41.9	37.8	0.63	n.s.
Last month	12.0	10.1	0.35	n.s.
Last week	6.3	3.6	1.37	n.s.
Cigarette smoking ([b])	21.2	17.4	0.86	n.s.

NB:
([a]) Alcohol use = more than one sip of beer, wine, vodka or champagne.
([b]) Any use of cigarettes.
n.s. = not significant.
p = level of significance.

tions using the six main scales suggested a significant reduction in alcohol use ($p < 0.02$) and intention to drink ($p < 0.03$) among students in the intervention group. The programme was also effective in increasing pupils' knowledge about the consequences of alcohol drinking ($p < 0.001$) and parent–child communication about the effects of both alcohol and cigarette use ($p < 0.03$). There were no significant divergences on two scales concerning peer norms and resistance skills (see Table 4). In addition, the results based on a single item suggested a reduction in the frequency of cigarette smoking ($f = 4.09$; $p < 0.05$) among the intervention group.

Because of the significant defects in programme delivery in three classes, additional analyses were conducted to check whether these problems might have produced negative side effects. Results of these additional analyses suggested that in one of the classes undesirable side effects could have occurred in teacher–parent cooperation.

Lessons learned

Evaluation demonstrated that administering the prevention programme via booklets from classrooms to families is a very effective way of involving parents in drug-prevention activities aimed at children aged 11 to 12. With 80 to 90 % of parents participating in one or more parent–child activity, this method is much more effective than more traditional ones, such as training in parenting skills or workshop activities organised in schools (Ferrer-Perez, 1994). However, in Poland, cooperation between schools and parents is a very sensitive component of the programme and should be carefully planned. The majority of parents should consent to the use of the programme before it begins which entails making available accurate information about the programme content, organisation and expected results. In addition, pupils whose parents do not participate in home activities require individual care and, if necessary, a 'parent substitute' from the school staff.

Using elected and trained peer leaders in the classroom activities was both feasible and well received by teachers and pupils alike, suggesting that peer leadership based to some extent on popularity is accepted among this age group in Polish schools. These results were similar to US experiences with elected and trained peer leaders of the same age in health-promotion programmes (Klepp et Al., 1986). However, cooperation between peer leaders and teachers is a fairly new idea in Polish schools, and teachers tend to have their own opinion about the ability of their students to play such a role. This probably explains why some teachers wanted more influence on the selection of peer leaders. Problems of competition between candidates reported by some teachers could no doubt be reduced by using a selection procedure in which pupils would not be told beforehand that they were selecting peer leaders. This procedure should be better explained during teacher training.

The study also emphasised the role of qualitative evaluation methods during the cross-cultural adaptation of a drug-prevention programme and the assessment of its effectiveness. For example, group interviews with teachers allowed the programme staff to understand the barriers in school–parent cooperation which was crucial for developing adequate solutions.

Table 4: Comparison of students in the intervention and reference groups on six main scales

Scale	Conditions	Mean		df	F-statistics	p
		Intervention n = 174	Reference n = 151			
Alcohol use (0–2)	pre-test	2.56	2.09	1	5.54	p < 0.02
	post-test	2.94	3.07	323	+	
		n = 168	n = 156			
Intention to use alcohol (0–12)	pre-test	2.33	2.06	1	5.28	p < 0.03
	post-test	2.77	3.17	322	+	
Peer norms (0–18)	pre-test	1.23	1.03	1	2.78	n.s.
	post-test	1.71	2.14	322	+	
Parent–child communication (0–3)	pre-test	1.99	2.24	1	4.99	p < 0.03
	post-test	2.32	2.30	322	+	
Perceived resistance skills (0–20)	pre-test	1.43	1.82	1	0.09	n.s.
	post-test	2.05	2.56	322	+	
Alcohol-related knowledge (0–5)	pre-test	2.85	2.92	1	25.20	p < 0.0001
	post-test	3.51	2.91	322	+	
Cumulative effect for the five scales				s = 1 m = 11/2 n = 158	6.81 +	p < 0.001

NB:
Numbers in parentheses indicate the range of values for each scale.
+ = changes in expected direction.
df = degree of freedom.
p = level of significance.
n.s. = not significant.

Conclusions

Although positive evaluation results mean that use of the programme in local-community alcohol-prevention initiatives can be recommended, defects in routine implementation may impair its effectiveness or even cause undesirable side effects. To ensure the quality of the programme delivery, teacher training is needed as well as simple evaluation standards to be used during routine implementation. According to the process evaluation results, the following aspects of programme implementation should be monitored:

- rates of parent–child booklet activities (with an expected 80 to 90 % of students working with parents on three to four booklets);
- rates of parental participation in the family evening event (with an expected 50 to 60 % of parents attending);
- rates of student satisfaction (with over 60 % of pupils being highly or very highly satisfied).

Most drug-prevention studies have to deal with common methodological problems concerning statistical analyses, measurement procedures, comparability of groups and attrition rates (National Institute on Alcohol Abuse and Alcoholism, 1997). While several of these problems seem to have been adequately addressed in the Polish study, some important limitations need to be mentioned here. The most significant constraints were the lack of any delay between the end of the intervention and follow-up, the relatively small sample and the problem of units of analysis. The statistical methods used in the individual-level prevention studies require the same units to be assigned to experimental conditions as are used in the analyses. In the Polish study, this was not possible because of the small sample. As a result, a school was used as a unit of randomisation and an individual as a unit of statistical analysis. It is worth noting that almost all of these problems were caused by serious limitations in funding.

References

Botvin, G., Baker, E., Filazzola, A., Botvin, E. (1990), 'A cognitive-behavioral approach to substance abuse prevention: one year follow-up', *Addictive Behaviour*, No 15, pp. 47–63.

Ferrer-Perez, X. (1994), 'Training of parents in prevention of drug abuse — 1994. Summary of a research report', paper presented at the conference 'The family and the prevention of drug dependence: strategies and models of approach', Warsaw, December.

Johnston, L., O'Malley, P., Bachman, J. (1993), *National survey results on drug use from the Monitoring the Future study, 1975–92*, Rockville, MD, National Institute on Drug Abuse.

Klepp, K., Halper, A., Perry, C. L. (1986), 'The efficacy of peer leaders in drug abuse prevention', *Journal of School Health*, No 56, pp. 407–11.

Komro, K., Perry, C., Veblen-Mortenson, S., Williams, C. (1994), 'Peer participation in Project Northland: a community-wide alcohol use prevention project', *Journal of School Health*, No 64, pp. 318–22.

National Institute on Alcohol Abuse and Alcoholism (1997), *Ninth special report to the US Congress on alcohol and health*, Bethesda, MD, NIAAA, pp. 301–27.

Ostaszewski, K., Bobrowski, K., Borucka, A., Okulicz-Kozaryn, K., Pisarska, A. (1999), 'Ocena funkcjonowania i skuteczności programu wczesnej profilaktyki alkoholowej "Program Domowych Detektywów"' ('Process and outcome evaluation of the alcohol primary prevention programme "Program Domowych Detektywów"'), unpublished manuscript, Institute of Psychiatry and Neurology, Warsaw.

Ostaszewski, K., Bobrowski, K., Borucka, A., Okulicz-Kozaryn, K., Pisarska, A., Perry, C., Williams, C. (1998), 'Program Domowych Detektywów. Adaptacja amerykanskiego programu profilaktyki alkoholowej dla mlodziezy we wczesnym okresie dojrzewania' ('A Polish adaptation of the US alcohol primary prevention programme for young adolescents'), *Alkoholizm i Narkomania*, No 3, pp. 339–60.

Perry, C., Williams, C., Veblen-Mortenson, S., Toomey, T., Komro, K., Anstine, P., McGovern, P., Finnegan, J., Forster, J., Wagenaar, A.,. Wolfson, M. (1996), 'Outcomes of a community-wide alcohol use prevention program during early adolescence: Project Northland', *American Journal of Public Health*, No 86, pp. 956–65.

Perry, C., Williams, C., Forster J., Wolfson, M., Wagenaar, A., Finnegan J., McGovern P., Velben-Mortenson S., Komro K., Anstine P. (1993), 'Background, conceptualisation, and design of a community-wide research program on adolescent alcohol use: Project Northland', *Health Education Research*, No 8, pp. 125–36.

Perry, C., Grant, M., Ernberg, G., Florenzano, R., Langdon, C., Myeni, A., Waahlberg, R., Berg, S., Andersson, K., Fisher, J., Blaze-Temple, D., Cross, D., Saunders, B., Jacobs, D., Schmid, T. (1989), 'WHO collaborative study on alcohol education and young people: outcomes of a four-country pilot study', *International Journal of the Addictions*, No 24, pp. 1145–171.

Rohrbach, L., Hodgson, C., Broder, B., Montgomery, S., Flay, B., Hansen, W., Pentz, M. (1995), 'Parental participation in drug abuse prevention: results from the Midwestern Prevention Project', in Boyd, G., Howard, J., Zucker, R. (Eds), *Alcohol problems among adolescents: current directions in prevention research,* Hillsdale, NJ, Lawrence Erlbaum, pp. 173–95.

Schaps, E., DiBartolo, R., Moskowitz, J., Palley, C., Churgin, S. (1981), 'A review of 127 drug abuse prevention program evaluations', *Journal of Drug Issues,* No 11, pp. 17–43.

Sieroslawski, J. (1997), 'Ile ich jest w rodzinach z problemem alkoholowym?' ('How many are there in families with alcohol-related problems?') *Świat Problemów,* No 2, pp. 12–14.

Tobler, N. (1986), 'Meta-analysis of 143 adolescent drug-prevention programs: quantitative outcome results of program participants compared to control or comparison group', *Journal of Drug Issues,* No 16, pp. 537–67.

Toomey, T., Williams, C., Perry, C., Murray, D., Dudovitz, B., Veblen-Mortenson, S. (1997), 'An alcohol primary prevention program for parents of 7th graders: the Amazing Alternatives! Home Program', *Journal on Child and Adolescent Substance Abuse,* No 5, pp. 35–53.

Uhl, A. (1998), 'Evaluation of primary prevention in the field of illicit drugs: definitions — concepts — problems', in Springer, A., Uhl, A. (Eds), *Evaluation research in regard to primary prevention of drug abuse,* Brussels, European Commission, pp. 171–74.

Williams, C. L., Perry, C. L., Farbakhsh, K., Veblen Mortenson, S. (1999), 'Project Northland: comprehensive alcohol use prevention for young adolescents, their parents, schools, peers, and communities', *Journal of Studies on Alcohol,* supplement 13, pp. 112–24.

Williams, C., Perry, C. (1998), 'Design and implementation of parent programs for a community-wide adolescent alcohol use prevention program', *Journal of Prevention and Intervention in the Community,* No 17, pp. 65–80.

Williams, C., Perry, C., Dudovitz, B., Veblen-Mortenson, S., Anstine, P., Komro, K. A., Toomey, T. L. (1995a), 'A home-based prevention program for sixth-grade alcohol use: results from Project Northland', *Journal of Primary Prevention,* No 16, pp. 125–47.

Williams, C., Toomey, T., McGovern, P., Wagenaar, A., Perry, C. (1995b), 'Development, reliability, and validity of self-report alcohol-use measures with young adolescents', *Journal on Child and Adolescent Substance Abuse,* No 4, pp. 17–40.

CHAPTER 8

REVIEWING THE PREVENTION OF RECREATIONAL DRUG USE

Amador Calafat

Characteristics and significance of recreational drug use

Over the last decade, recreational drug use has become one of the most widespread forms of drug consumption and a major concern in Europe. At the same time, other more traditional forms of drug use — such as heroin use — have become more contained. Although recreational or weekend drug consumption mainly involves alcohol and tobacco, other illicit substances are also widely taken, especially cannabis. Cannabis use has become very prevalent in much of Europe, irrespective of its legal position in the individual Member States, and is followed in popularity by ecstasy, amphetamines and cocaine.

The rise in use of certain drugs in recreational settings has coincided with the rapid expansion of what might be called 'recreational culture' throughout western Europe. Characteristic of this culture is the significant increase in the range of entertainments the leisure industry offers to young people, not only in terms of the number of entertainment venues and activities, but also of the much greater availability of time. 'House' and other dance music is one of the defining styles of this development, and the importance of 'raves' in shaping this recreational culture — albeit not to the same extent in all countries — cannot be ignored.

To address drug use so closely linked to a cultural movement requires understanding and action at different levels and from different perspectives. In the recreational context, these include:

- considering the entire recreational scene as a dangerous form of drug promotion and urging campaigns to modify it and restrict its further expansion;
- accepting that alcohol and drug consumption is an established fact in recreational environments which it is futile to try to restrict, and that the most urgently needed and effective approach is to provide accurate information to help reduce problem consumption and its associated behaviour among current consumers;
- understanding that the recreational scene is a specific culture, which has positive effects on young people's self-expression, social skills and maturity, but one that has to be studied in order to understand the many factors involved.

Although alcohol, tobacco and cannabis are still the most widely used substances in Europe, ecstasy is more typical than any other drug of this new era of recreational use. Ecstasy refers not only to one specific chemical compound — 3,4-methylene-dioxy-N-methylamphetamine (MDMA) — but also to other related substances that are consumed under this generic name. Ecstasy has become a symbol of some of the most distinctive values of this recreational culture, including a certain type of music and dancing and a way of establishing relationships.

The rapid spread of ecstasy has been enhanced by the properties attributed to it. It was perceived at the end of the 1980s and early 1990s as being a relatively or completely harmless drug, encouraging contact between people at an affordable price, although it was also acknowledged to be incompatible with the use of other substances, especially alcohol. For many people, including some professionals in the drugs field, the apparent absence of side effects associated with ecstasy and the possibility of avoiding them by taking certain preventive steps (drinking water, resting from time to time and not mixing ecstasy with other substances) created the illusion that, used intelligently, the drug could be consumed without ill effects. All that was necessary, then, was to provide young people with sufficient information to ensure that they took the necessary precautions. If on-site testing could also demonstrate that the tablets used were not adulterated — a preventive measure already introduced in some European countries — where was the risk? Yet clinical and epidemiological facts, ethnographic studies and tests carried out on both animals and human beings have shown that ecstasy is not such a harmless drug after all.

The Sonar project, undertaken by the Institut de Recherches Européen sur les Facteurs de Risque chez l'Enfant et l'Adolescent (Irefrea) with the financial support of the European Commission, has, since 1996, been studying the issues and problems associated with drug use by young people in recreational environments. The study is being carried out in towns and cities in nine European countries [34]. To date, the Sonar project has identified the diversity of forms of drug consumption in urban areas, the various subgroups involved, differences between Member States and the cultural characteristics associated with drug use. It has also provided information on some forms of risk behaviour and risk perception. These data (Calafat et al., 1998, 1999) can help to focus preventive policies more effectively as well as pointing the way for future studies [35].

Some of the conclusions of the Irefrea study (Calafat et al., 1998) were obtained from a sample of 1 627 young people who habitually participate in weekend recreational activities in five European cities [36]. Approximately half of these young people served as a control group to increase the validity of the findings. According to this research, ecstasy users:

- are more likely to be multiple substance users than other young people who go out at night (control group);
- are more likely to indulge in abusive consumption (for example, get drunk more frequently);

(34) Germany, Greece, Spain, France, Italy, Netherlands, Austria, Portugal and the UK.
(35) These reports can be downloaded from (http://www.irefrea.org).
(36) Coimbra, Modena, Nice, Palma de Mallorca and Utrecht.

- are not marginalised individuals, but do exhibit certain differences from the control group, such as being more likely to be sensation seekers or to exhibit behaviour symptomatic of greater social deviance, such as petty theft or fighting;
- tend not to consider ecstasy use as particularly risky and to have a more positive view of its effects;
- are less interested in prevention;
- have a greater interest in dance culture.

The fact that ecstasy users are less interested in preventive issues is important since understanding their attitude towards prevention will help to target preventive activities more effectively and provide a clearer understanding of what they can be expected to achieve. A key factor for ecstasy users' lack of interest in prevention is that they want to experience the drug's effects, which they view favourably, and they therefore underestimate its possible risks. For example, in Coimbra — and similar figures are found in other cities — 26 % of non-users believe that ecstasy is addictive, compared to 1 % of users. In Utrecht — and, again, similar figures are found in other cities — the unpredictable effects of ecstasy are a cause of concern to 38 % of non-users, but to only 17 % of users. If, for example, the young people of Palma de Mallorca are asked how important it is for them to know the chemical composition of the 'ecstasy' they use, 33 % attach no importance at all to it, 55 % say that they would be interested but that they use the tablets without any problems, and only 11 % say that if they did not know the composition of the tablet they would 'prefer' not to take it.

This 'anti-preventive' attitude is not surprising since the very concept of leisure time involves a certain disregard for rules and an indulgence in risk behaviour. Of the sample of 2 700 young people questioned during 1998 (Calafat et al., 1999), 60.8% reported being drunk at least once a month. In so doing, they accepted a high level of risk, demonstrated by the fact that 43 % had driven under the influence of alcohol and 30 % under the influence of another drug. Of those who had driven under the influence of alcohol, 13.7 % had been fined for doing so, 13.4 % had been involved in road accidents and 6 % had been arrested.

Yet experiencing problems associated with drug use is often not sufficient reason to give them up, and among the same sample 29 % admitted having continued to use a particular drug despite encountering problems with it. In most cases, the drug that caused the majority of problems was alcohol (36.9 %), followed by cannabis (19.9%) and ecstasy (14.0 %). Ultimately, it would appear that being a user automatically reduces receptiveness towards prevention. This attitude is influenced by many different elements, including the fact that initial experiences of a drug are relatively easy to handle, or that being a user makes it necessary to create an intellectual mechanism to justify such behaviour, not forgetting the fact that the existence of risks may actually be regarded as a positive factor by the user.

Preventing recreational drug use

At present, preventing recreational drug use is a relatively new and underdeveloped field, and one which presents many challenges, both theoretical and practical. The deep concern generated in Europe over the past 15 years by the scale of the recreational phenomenon and the appearance of substances such as ecstasy in this context has made finding an appropriate preventive approach to these forms of drug use and the circumstances in which they arise a matter of urgency.

Traditionally, drug-prevention programmes have focused mainly on schools, and an extensive body of experience exists, with a number of programmes already evaluated. However, these programmes, which require relatively stable and definable conditions since they involve a specific group (for example, pupils of the same age sharing part of their timetable), cannot necessarily be adopted in broader settings. Instead, preventing recreational drug use requires a full understanding of a very potent, highly developed and ever-changing youth culture, within which drugs have an important place and are often seen as powerful symbols. Community prevention, although it has been less studied, may come closer to providing the methods and instruments needed for preventing recreational drug use. Be that as it may, the past successes, failures and evaluations of drug prevention must not be overlooked.

Nevertheless, the form of prevention that has rather unexpectedly developed to contain the problems associated with recreational drug use has little in common with more traditional drug-prevention approaches. Various factors have influenced the type of initiative that has been growing up in many European cities and countries. One important phenomenon has been the popularity of ecstasy, the social factors associated with its use (such as the popularity of dance and 'house' music, the belief that it is a modern and 'safe' drug) and the initial lack of awareness of its harmful effects, together with the belief that the few problems that had been identified and accepted could easily be controlled by taking certain precautions. An associated issue is the recent success of damage-limitation policies in the field of treatment, which has prompted thoughts of a similar approach in the area of recreational drug use.

'Damage-limitation' prevention is based on the assumption that a large proportion of the problems associated with recreational drug use could be controlled if the person concerned was aware of them and took the appropriate preventive steps (for example, drinking plenty of water or resting from time to time). The preventive activity would thus involve providing the user with the necessary information to make the right decisions. From this angle, the problem would not be the drug consumption itself — regarded as inevitable in any case, and an established social fact — but ignorance of what action to take to deal with its consequences.

This transposition of the principles of damage limitation used in drug treatment to the prevention field, however, is not without its problems. Damage limitation in treatment is aimed at individuals who are deeply involved in drug use, whose lives are powerfully conditioned by it, and who have very limited ability to make decisions about their own lives. Any expectation that they would abandon or greatly reduce their consumption of the drugs on which they are dependent is, in many cases, illusory. The circumstances and characteristics of young people in recreational environments are very far from this stereotype. This target group represents a wide spectrum of young people with a generally high level of control over broad areas of their lives who use drugs to varying degrees, from abstinence to dependence.

Introducing elements of risk reduction into the preventive measures targeted at these young people seems to be the most appropriate approach. It is consistent with a value system in which individual responsibility for actions is increasingly more important than a paternalistic approach. However, it seems neither very logical nor consistent with the evidence to rely on this approach as the main, or in some cases only, drug-prevention strategy. The capacity of these users to manage the risks they are taking, as well as their interest in avoiding the problems associated with such drug use, has tended to be overestimated. As a result, campaigns have generally involved distributing information leaflets, attractively presented and in tune with youth culture, in the hope that young people will learn to use certain specific drugs in a less dangerous way.

In practice, this has been the most frequent type of preventive measure for recreational drug use. A recent review of current preventive programmes in European recreational settings (Burkhart, 1999) notes that the majority of such initiatives are based on providing information and that, contrary to what they supposedly claim, most of the people at whom these programmes are targeted are abstainers or occasional rather than frequent users. This whole range of measures has therefore been implemented without proper evaluation and without taking into account the failure — as far back as the 1960s — of school drug-prevention initiatives based solely on information.

Those responsible for these programmes have even taken a belligerent attitude towards more 'traditional' prevention approaches, regarding them as ineffectual and not reaching the heart of the problem. They view recreational drug use by young people as an established fact about which nothing can be done. In their view, preventive efforts should not attempt to influence trends, but should confine themselves to ensuring that recreational consumption does not become a problem for the individual or the group. As a result, there have been no serious evaluations of the effects of these campaigns —- which are directed at consumers — on non- or occasional users.

While the experiences and views of practitioners in the field are clearly important in planning drug-prevention policies, such professionals may be biased in their statements, especially regarding ideological aspects. There can be no doubt that, in the drugs field, where many different views co-exist, ideological perspectives are significant. This, of course, is no bad thing, provided that it remains possible, in discussions or in the approaches adopted, to differentiate between facts for which some empirical basis exists and personal beliefs.

A good illustration of how such confusion can occur is found in a recent study which examined the drug-prevention strategies preferred by 1 200 Spanish primary-

and secondary-school teachers (Mejías et al., 1999). Encouraging self-esteem, responsibility and independence was favoured by 50 %. A very close second was value clarification (45 %), while the least popular strategy was training in social skills (16%). A review of 58 longitudinal studies of the aetiology of drug use (Petraitis et al., 1998) shows that 11 out of 12 studies find no relationship between low self-esteem and continuing drug use, nor between anxiety or depression and drug use.

While low self-esteem is perhaps more a consequence than a cause of substance abuse, nine studies did find a relationship between future drug use and extroversion, assertiveness, lack of inhibition and sensation seeking, while only two did not. What can have occurred to produce such a misunderstanding? The assumption is that teachers defend the educational ideal, which does not necessarily coincide — and, as this study clearly shows, does not in fact coincide — with the objectives of drug prevention.

Why are teachers so unenthusiastic about interactive programmes that teach social skills when in practice these are often the only ones that actually have preventive effects (Tobler, 1997)? After all, the most effective initiatives are those that attempt to motivate young people actively instead of making them passive receptacles for information. Various reasons can be posited for the teachers' response, including ignorance, the greater complexity involved in implementing interactive programmes, or the fact that such programmes require training or skills that the teachers may not be able to provide. The basic reason, however, is that teachers have greater confidence in programmes which are more in tune with their educational beliefs. If drug-prevention in schools 30 years ago demonstrated the serious limitations of information provision as a method, even when aimed at a fairly receptive population which pupils are by definition, how can current approaches based almost exclusively on providing information — and to young people who have little interest in drug prevention and in some cases are deeply involved in drug abuse (Calafat et al., 1998, 1999) — be expected to succeed?

Future action

The range of possible options for action is currently fairly broad, although most of the drug-prevention programmes that have been proposed in recreational settings have concentrated on providing information to users or testing the composition of tablets to avoid adulteration. Instead, action should focus on controlling supply and demand. Experience of drug prevention shows that establishing coordinated strategies at different levels increases the potential for success. Among the areas for focus are:

- accessibility to drugs;
- legal or police pressure;
- risk perception;
- risk limitation;
- group (or environmental) expectations and pressure;
- prior experiences with drugs, risks and problems;

- levels of intelligence, personal abilities and expectations;
- a culture which supports or justifies young people's behaviour.

Primary prevention — whether in schools, the family or the community — is not a thing of the past, but remains very important, especially when young people are being initiated into recreational practices and high-risk behaviour at a very early age([37]). In addition to primary prevention, the following measures can be implemented:

- self-help and peer-group pressure;
- repressive action;
- providing information on risks to users;
- testing the substances consumed;
- promoting safer dance parties;
- outreach campaigns;
- information campaigns;
- increasing the provision and expertise of emergency services;
- alternative drug-free recreational activities;
- influencing the recreational scene to promote health advancement.

Some of these measures are already being effectively practised in various EU Member States. In the Netherlands and the UK, for example, night-club security staff are given special training, public transport is provided at night, clubs ensure easy access to contraceptive vending machines and drinking water, and so on.

Control measures, such as observing closing times or complying with legislation on minors, have been established to a greater or lesser extent in all EU countries, although in practice the level of tolerance to recreational drug use is quite high. Some programmes already attempt to deal specifically with the problems of recreational substance use. In Sweden, a special police division has been formed to identify and penalise young people whose recreational drug use is problematic. Measures to regulate entertainment venues are difficult to enforce in many countries and cities, particularly given the many vested interests involved, above all in the leisure industry. A field study undertaken by Irefrea (Calafat et al, 1999) in 1998 in nine European cities ([38]) found a generally low police presence in entertainment districts, while the private security staff employed by the venues themselves were more prominent.

The search for alternative forms of weekend entertainment to bars and clubs, as has begun in some Spanish cities such as Gijón, may be an important recourse, provided that these alternative entertainments are set up on a serious basis and as long-term projects. It is common in the drug-prevention field to see schemes established with virtually no continuity. Some self-help and self-motivation initiatives have been set up — for example in Manchester and some German towns — by the same young people who are experiencing problems with drug use.

([37]) For more on drug prevention within the family, see Mendes et al. (1999), available at (http://www.irefrea.org).

([38]) Athens, Berlin, Coimbra, Manchester, Modena, Nice, Palma de Mallorca, Utrecht and Vienna.

Conclusions

Given the recent rapid growth in recreational drug use, it would appear important to devote some resources to defining the entertainment and recreational culture. This is not an easy matter, but it is important to understand that this new phenomenon involves many other elements than simply the interests of young people, the most significant of which are the financial interests of the leisure industry itself.

Information leaflets do, of course, have their place within prevention strategies aimed at recreational drug use, but they will need more clearly defined objectives, content and target groups, and greater cooperation with other drug-prevention programmes. The information which such leaflets have supplied hitherto has tended to focus on advice on how best to confront and solve the problems caused by recreational drug use which, even in the best-case scenario, is a limited objective. This is because users in these environments have only a partial interest in preventive measures and, even when they do show interest, information alone does not appear to influence them to reduce their drug use. In a study of the reasons for increases and decreases in the use of various drugs among the US population, undertaken from 1976 to 1996 (Johnston and O'Malley, 1998), certain factors — such as continuity of studies, participation in antisocial activities, number of outlets — were found to be reliable predictors of drug use. The only factor that really explained the historical changes, year by year, however, was the perceived risk or disapproval of a particular drug.

Recreational drug use is clearly a priority area for preventive action and its importance can only continue to increase. It is now time to find the most appropriate approach to this phenomenon.

References

Burkhart, G. (1999), 'New study on synthetic drugs', *DrugNet Europe*, No 20, p. 2.

Calafat, A., Bohrn, K., Juan, M., Kokkevi, A., Maalsté, N., et al. (1999), *Night life in Europe and recreative drug use*: *Sonar 98*, Palma de Mallorca, Irefrea.

Calafat, A., Stocco, P., Mendes, F., Simon, J., van de Wijngaart, G., Sureda, P., et al. (1998), *Characteristics and social representation of ecstasy in Europe*, Palma de Mallorca, Irefrea.

Johnston, L. D., O'Malley, P. M. (1998), 'Explaining recent increases in students' marijuana use: impact of perceived risks and disapproval, 1976 through 1996', *American Journal of Public Health*, No 8, pp. 887–92.

Mejías, E., Comas, D., Elso, J., Navarro, J., Vega, A. (1999), *Los docentes españoles y la prevención del consumo de drogas (Spanish teachers and prevention of drug use)*, Madrid, Fundación de Ayuda Contra la Drogadicción.

Petraitis, J., Flay, B. R., Miller, T. D., Torpy, E. J., Greiner, B. (1998), 'Illicit substance use among adolescents: a matrix of prospective predictors', *Substance Use and Misuse*, No 33, pp. 2561–604.

Tobler, N. S. (1997), 'Meta-analysis of adolescence drug-prevention programs: results of the 1993 meta-analysis', in Bukoski , W. J., (Ed.), *Meta-analysis of drug abuse prevention programs*, Rockville, MD, National Institute on Drug Abuse, pp. 5–68.

Further reading

Mendes, F., Relvas, P., Lourenço, M., Recio, J. L., et al. (1999), *Family relationships and primary prevention of drug use in early adolescence*, Palma de Mallorca, Irefrea.

Part III

Improving evaluation practice

INTRODUCTION

In Chapter 9, Pavel Bem sketches the overall development of, and trends in, drug prevention in central and eastern Europe and draws parallels with developments in the European Union. The author divides the central and east European countries into three categories and identifies the specific needs of each of these groups.

Relations between the 'research world' and the 'political world', as well as the communication and interaction between them, are the focus of Chapter 10. Susanne Schardt draws on her own involvement in the European Cities on Drug Policy network and her work in the Drug Policy Coordination Office of the City of Frankfurt and gives advice on how best to transmit scientific research findings to politicians and decision-makers.

In Chapter 11, Teresa Salvador-Llivina examines the rationale and objectives behind the EMCDDA's Exchange on drug demand-reduction action (EDDRA) information system. She traces its background, describing the various stages involved in developing and testing the prototype, and presents the key recommendations from the feasibility phase.

Philippe Roux continues the story of EDDRA in Chapter 12 by highlighting the system's current status. He describes the processes of information gathering, quality control and maintenance of the system, as well as the roles of the various partners involved. The author demonstrates both the technical and scientific challenges inherent in the EDDRA project, and examines areas for future development.

In Chapter 13, Sabine Haas discusses how best to convey the importance of evaluation, as well as the practical skills required, to drug-prevention practitioners. Reporting on experiences in Austria, she highlights the need for clearly defined objectives in planning evaluation, and describes the methods used to develop practical expertise. She concludes by proposing concrete ways of supporting the implementation of evaluation at European level.

Taking the work of the Réseau SécuCités-Drogues network as a starting point, Joana Judice focuses on drug prevention in local communities in Chapter 14. Using examples of drug-prevention projects targeting young people in Barcelona and Saint-Herblain, she describes the context in which these programmes were created, the evaluation of the initiatives and the obstacles this evaluation revealed. The author concludes by outlining the characteristics of good practice at local level, while also highlighting the importance of adequate funding.

In Chapter 15, Alfred Uhl explores the limits and constraints of evaluation studies in general. He outlines a number of common problems, including imprecise terminology and inadequate methodologies, and suggests ways of overcoming them, while also underlining that there are no easy or definitive solutions to such problems. Instead, concerted action is required to improve the quality of both drug prevention and evaluation in Europe.

CHAPTER 9

EVALUATING DRUG PREVENTION IN CENTRAL AND EASTERN EUROPE

Pavel Bem

The 1990s were a period of dramatic social, political and economic changes in central and eastern Europe. In the wake of these developments, many central and east European countries (CEECs) were confronted by unprecedented growth in illicit drug use, especially among adolescents and young people. Drug-related crime and new threats to public health — including those posed by intravenous drug use, the spread of HIV/AIDS and hepatitis B and C — have been the inevitable consequences of this emerging social phenomenon.

Many of the CEECs are attempting to tackle these problems with no national drug demand-reduction policies, with no established drug-prevention and treatment system and with serious limits to the public-health resources available to them. As a result, all these countries must maximise the effectiveness of the resources used and the interventions implemented. The need for cost-effective primary-prevention responses, as well as treatment and rehabilitation, is becoming a crucial issue for both national drug demand-reduction strategies and local public-health policy planning.

Since the early 1990s, a great number of preventive and treatment interventions have been initiated in almost all the countries of the region. In some cases, the need was so urgent that the programmes were established with no prior evidence of their effectiveness. However, research has demonstrated that maintaining such programmes without adequate knowledge of whether or not their approach is effective is fundamentally problematic and may even be counterproductive. Empirical evidence of the value or cost-effectiveness of individual drug demand-reduction programmes, as well as of national demand-reduction strategies, is thus essential for policy planning.

Current status of drug-prevention evaluation

In reviewing the current status of drug-prevention evaluation research and practice in central and eastern Europe it is clear that, although the importance of evaluation research is widely recognised throughout the region, it is not sufficiently implemented in practice in most CEECs.

Central and eastern Europe is a very heterogeneous region which is defined more from a geopolitical than from an economic, social or public-health perspective. In addition, the level of drug abuse varies greatly from country to country, despite some commonly reported regional trends. The current level of development in drug demand reduction, the extent of the services available, as well as the institutional and human capacities involved in the field, differ even more dramatically. Thus, in assessing the current status of drug-prevention evaluation in the region, major, sometimes even extreme, variations are apparent.

A significant amount of documentation and information about drug demand reduction in the CEECs has been collected since systematic and comprehensive international assistance became available in the 1990s, for example from the EU Phare multi-beneficiary drugs programme, from the Pompidou Group of the Council of Europe or from the World Health Organisation. In the context of the Phare project on drug information systems (DIS) and the Phare project on technical assistance to drug demand reduction ([39]), the Phare Programme Coordination Unit (PCU) in Riga has generated comprehensive reports on each CEEC describing the status of various aspects of drug demand reduction as well as the specific needs of each country (National Reports, 1998; Summary Reports, 1999).

The Phare multi-beneficiary drugs programme has assessed the status of evaluation in the partner countries by asking its network of drug demand-reduction coordinators the following questions ([40]).

- Does your country carry out evaluation and drug-prevention research?
- Do evaluation and drug-prevention practice take place in your country?
- Does your country have an evaluation and drug-prevention policy?
- Is your country familiar with the EMCDDA *Guidelines for the evaluation of drug prevention* (EMCDDA, 1998)? ([41])
- Is your country familiar with the EMCDDA's Exchange on drug demand-reduction action (EDDRA) information system? ([42])
- What are the drug-prevention evaluation needs of your country?

From the results of this assessment, the CEECs can be grouped into three main clusters.

- Countries in which drug demand reduction is well developed, based on:
  - existing and operational demand-reduction strategies;
  - a wide range of available drug-prevention and treatment services;
  - guaranteed permanent national and local funding;
  - minimum quality-assurance instruments in place.

([39]) Information on the Phare multi-beneficiary drugs programme is available at (http://www.fad.phare.org/). Information on the Phare project on drug information systems is available at (http://www.fad.phare.org/dis/). Information on the Phare project on technical assistance to drug demand reduction is available at (http://www.fad.phare.org/ddr/).

([40]) The Phare partner countries are Albania, Bosnia-Herzegovina, Bulgaria, Czech Republic, Estonia, Former Yugoslav Republic of Macedonia (FYROM), Hungary, Latvia, Lithuania, Poland, Romania, Slovakia and Slovenia.

([41]) For more information on the *Guidelines for the evaluation of drug prevention*, see Chapters 5 and 6.

([42]) For more information on the EDDRA information system, see Chapters 11 and 12.

- Countries in which drug demand reduction is fairly well developed, based on:
  - existing, but not fully operational demand-reduction strategies;
  - available, but limited drug-prevention and treatment services;
  - some, but insufficient, national or local funding;
  - no quality-assurance instruments in place.
- Countries in which drug demand reduction is less well developed, based on:
  - no national demand-reduction strategy;
  - no or very limited demand-reduction services available;
  - no or very limited national demand-reduction funding;
  - no quality-assurance instruments in place.

Evaluation and drug-prevention research

The countries in the first group reported experience of evaluation and drug-prevention research, with Poland the most advanced in this context. In the Czech Republic, a study conducted in 1998 to evaluate the effectiveness of major primary-prevention programmes suggested that interactive and comprehensive drug-prevention projects were the most efficient. Research carried out in Slovenia from 1995 to 1997 evaluated over 80 primary-prevention school-based projects. Drug-prevention and evaluation studies have also been undertaken in Hungary and Slovakia.

The countries in clusters 2 and 3 had not carried out any evaluation or drug-prevention research.

Drug-prevention evaluation practice

In the Czech Republic, Hungary, Poland and Slovenia, evaluation is becoming an integral component of drug-prevention programmes and an obligatory condition for receiving government funds. However, even these countries reported that drug-prevention professionals had limited experience of evaluation practice, especially of methods and types of evaluation.

Countries in cluster 2 reported limited evaluation experience which is not an integral part of most of these countries' drug demand-reduction programmes. Some of these CEECs stated that international projects, such as the EU Phare project on technical assistance to drug demand reduction, had provided them with their first opportunity to introduce aspects of evaluation into drug-prevention practice in a planned and integrated way.

Countries in cluster 3 have almost no experience of evaluation methodology, and, where this does exist, it derives purely from international projects.

Evaluation and drug-prevention policy

Cluster 1 countries have an established evaluation policy and evaluation is a mandatory component of all programmes that request government (national or local) funds.

The drug demand-reduction strategies adopted by cluster 1 and 2 countries typically come under the umbrella of a comprehensive national drug policy. While almost all existing national drug strategies include some form of evaluation, this can hardly be interpreted in most cases as a comprehensive or sophisticated enough instrument to deliver what would be expected from a national drug-strategy evaluation.

Cluster 3 countries have no national evaluation or drug-prevention policy.

EMCDDA Guidelines for the evaluation of drug prevention

All cluster 1, 2 and 3 countries reported basic knowledge of the EMCDDA's *Guidelines for the evaluation of drug prevention,* although practical use of the manual differs markedly. Most CEECs do not use the guidelines in practice, although Lithuania has translated the document and distributed it widely throughout the country.

Awareness of EDDRA

All cluster 1, 2 and 3 countries reported basic knowledge of the EDDRA information system, although only very few stated that they had derived practical benefits from its use.

Drug-prevention evaluation needs

All CEECs reported an urgent need to implement drug-prevention evaluation much more widely. From analyses of the Phare country reports (National Reports, 1998; Summary Reports, 1999), it can be concluded that both common (regional) and individual (country-specific) needs in the area of drug-prevention evaluation exist in central and eastern Europe.

Common needs throughout the region include:

- training demand-reduction professionals and drug-prevention project managers in evaluation methodology and skills;
- developing and disseminating evaluation manuals and guidelines, which must be simple, comprehensive and cheap for practical use;
- sharing examples of good practice in successful demand-reduction projects in EU Member States as well as in the CEECs;
- training policy-makers in evaluation advocacy.

Country-specific needs include:

- clusters 1 and 2:
  - long-term assessment of the outcomes of primary-prevention projects;
  - evaluation of community-based drug-prevention programmes;
  - evaluation of mass-media campaigns;
  - evaluation of school-based drug-prevention programmes.

- cluster 3:
  - support in designing and implementing national demand-reduction policies;
  - support in funding drug-prevention programmes and evaluation research.

Conclusions

The variations in drug-prevention evaluation status among the individual CEECs are significant. While some countries are well advanced in this area and are approaching the level of EU Member States, others have very limited experience of evaluating demand-reduction projects. International programmes, such as the EU Phare initiatives, have proved in many cases to be pilot instruments and to have provided many CEECs with their first opportunity to integrate evaluation components into their demand-reduction activities.

Facilitating and reinforcing the integration of comprehensive evaluation methodology into drug-prevention programmes has been stressed as a priority in almost all CEECs, with training drug practitioners in evaluation skills the most commonly accepted method. The diversity of the countries in the region, however, has demonstrated the need to tailor international assistance to specific national needs. Taking into account the experience of drug-prevention evaluation in some CEECs, mutual information exchange between them should be promoted. Applying economic criteria and cost-effectiveness philosophy in drug-demand reduction is clearly another crucial element in responding to the growing drug problem in the region.

References

European Monitoring Centre for Drugs and Drug Addiction (1998), *Guidelines for the evaluation of drug prevention,* Manuals No 1, Lisbon, EMCDDA.

National Reports (1998), 'National reports on the drug situation in central and east European countries' (http://www.fad.phare.org/dis/natrep.html).

Summary Reports (1999), 'Summary reports on the drug situation in central and east European countries' (http://www.fad.phare.org/dis/natrep.html).

CHAPTER 10

COMMUNICATING RESEARCH FINDINGS TO POLICY-MAKERS

Susanne Schardt

The good news

Politicians constantly make use of evaluations and statistics, particularly in adopting, rejecting or legitimising specific political strategies. In order both to examine and to justify their actions, politicians strongly advocate ongoing evaluation of the impact of their policies on the public since, at local level in particular, such measures are directly at the mercy of public opinion.

In the context of drug prevention, comparing local strategies with those implemented in other local authorities is particularly important, and it is here that a society's ability to reach a consensus on, and to provide, an efficient response to public health and safety issues comes to the fore. Economic aspects, too, have long played a major role in formulating drug policy. With an increasingly limited budget, local authorities tend to focus on measures that are both comparatively cheap and that have an immediate and visible impact. Many so-called 'harm-reduction' measures — such as needle-exchange programmes, 'users' rooms (where drugs can be taken under safe and hygienic conditions), or methadone-maintenance programmes — have been implemented not only because they help the individual drug user, but also because they have a positive impact on public order and safety and thus benefit the local community as a whole.

The bad news

On the other hand, politicians generally do not have first-hand professional experience in their particular fields of responsibility and research considerations are not necessarily the prime determining factors in their decision-making. Instead, their decisions tend to be based on political (including party political) and economic factors, as well as on public opinion, which often only reaches politicians indirectly via the media.

Since politicians are often responsible for several different areas, they have little time to study research reports or to find the answer to pending problems in relevant scientific publications. Furthermore, analysing research findings has not yet been institutionalised at local-authority level. Although press-cutting departments have been set up by local governments to scan the media and pass on relevant information to politicians, they generally do not search scientific publications. Therefore, if scientific findings are being passed on to the politicians, it is mostly via the media. It is not, then, surprising that political decisions are much more frequently based on 'public' opinion than on scientific evaluation.

The greatly simplified use of research findings and data — for example, via the Internet — does offer some theoretical advantages in that it enables as much information as possible on relevant subjects to be relayed to decision-makers. In practice, however, local authorities tend to have only limited access to the Internet and its daily use as a reference tool is not yet sufficiently established. Furthermore, in most cases, the politicians themselves hardly use this technology at all. Here, too, the time factor plays a fairly significant role: as every user knows, the Internet can provide unlimited answers to questions that were never asked; conversely, finding a precise answer to a specific question can take a very long time.

In addition to most politicians' lack of professional expertise in their subject, their limited access to the relevant information available, and the fact that they anyway have little time to research their subject matter, many local authorities do not have the opportunity to 'adapt' evaluation research to a specific political activity. This is mostly due to the factors determining political decision-making mentioned above. Yet evaluation can clearly enhance drug policy. It can be used to examine and, above all, legitimise political measures, but will only very rarely give rise directly to new political decisions. This is because the actual implementation of certain measures is mostly guided by what is politically possible given constraints such as the balance of power, the need to find a political and social consensus in relevant committees or public opinion. In terms of priorities, scientific evaluation usually comes below these political necessities and is at best used to underline what has already been discussed and decided. Scientific data tend to have the greatest effect when communicated to politicians in a condensed form and when they refer to problems pending in the local community. Given that decision-makers are used to reading press clippings, 'bringing evaluation to the politicians' therefore requires a language and style which has more in common with journalistic principles than with pure research criteria. Lengthy, in-depth information is unlikely to be read and information must be kept 'straight and simple'. This is a challenge which scientific researchers must meet if their findings are to influence political decisions.

The above considerations are largely based on the author's own experience of working in the Drug Policy Coordination Office of the City of Frankfurt and with the European Cities on Drug Policy (ECDP) network during the past 10 years ([43]). Through its role as a drug-policy advisory and clearing body, the ECDP has made it its job to improve the exchange of information with local government. A recurrent question is: 'How can I get my message across to my local politician?'

Issues of cost effectiveness, whether or not a political consensus can be found for certain measures, as well as whether their impact will be visible to the public and be reflected positively in the media, should all be borne in mind. In so doing, it is

([43]) For more information on the ECDP network, see (http://www.ecdp.net/).

crucial to remember that, at political level, evaluation is used specifically to allow politicians to examine their own actions as simply and quickly as possible.

A crucial question in implementing as well as evaluating drug policy is whether the measure can actually change an existing problem. To communicate such a message effectively to political decision-makers, however, an overview of data is not enough. Instead, this data must be 'translated' into the possible political actions that can be taken.

Experience gained from the work of the ECDP has shown that the network's local-authority members are particularly interested in including more 'best-practice' models and in more extensive evaluation of drug-policy measures. The growing interest in evaluation in Europe makes it possible to compare the strategies of different local authorities and to draw conclusions from the effects of specific political measures. Furthermore, these methods help to accelerate the sometimes exceedingly laborious and lengthy process of developing drug policies and implementing them in real terms, since current experience can be used as a point of reference.

It goes without saying, however, that political strategies cannot simply be transferred from one local authority to the next. What works in one city may not work in another. Why this is so is clearly a very interesting subject for scientific evaluation, and one which would also be of great interest to politicians.

Use of EMCDDA products

The European Monitoring Centre for Drugs and Drug Addiction's *Annual report on the state of the drugs problem in the European Union* (EMCDDA, 1995, 1997, 1998, 1999) is an indispensable source of information for the ECDP network and a valuable reference work for local decision-makers. With the support of the EMCDDA, the ECDP for the first time distributed a copy of the annual report to the participants at its eighth International Cities Conference, 'Common initiatives in drug policy — an assessment of local drug problems, needs and strategies', held in Halle, Germany, in June 1999. Many of the politicians at the conference learned of the existence of this publication for the first time in this way, and their response was overwhelmingly positive.

The EMCDDA annual report, however, provides relatively little, if any, locally oriented information. This may be attributable to the fact that the information on which it is based is delivered by the national focal points of the Reitox network which include scant local data in their national reports, and sometimes none at all. Considerably better cooperation with local authorities would be most welcome here, particularly given that policy-making in Europe appears to be increasingly developing from the bottom up, giving local authorities a much greater role than before.

Local authority members of the ECDP almost consistently do not make use of the Exchange on drug demand-reduction action (EDDRA) information system and this is certainly due to the fact that the Internet has been little used in local government up to now ([44]). The EDDRA system could, however, play a significant role once the daily use of the Internet has become established in the public sector to the same extent that it already appears to have been established among most practitioners working in the field of drugs, research and medicine, and among most non-governmental organisations.

Conclusions

In conclusion, the following points can be made. First, it is important to make politicians aware of the utility, possibilities and limitations of evaluation.

Second, information should be provided to politicians with a specific goal in mind. It is crucial to circulate available research findings and present them to local government politicians on an active and regular basis, and not just to wait for politicians to make specific enquiries.

A major drawback to the use of research studies in politics is the poor comparability of data and the practically non-existent evaluation of overall political strategies, particularly at local-government level. This applies both to the EMCDDA's products and to most other research findings, which, furthermore, tend to be used only very sporadically or are largely unknown.

A scientifically based assessment of the effects of certain drug strategies would be desirable, as would the establishment of a set of instruments to facilitate continuous feedback, both on the part of practitioners working in the drugs field and politicians responsible for drug policy. In the same way as providing information to politicians, a proactive approach in requesting feedback would be useful. One way of facilitating this could be to organise a conference similar to the evaluation conference from which this monograph derives, where local politicians and local civil servants could speak about their experiences of using scientific findings in their everyday work. By describing their needs and requirements, some form of continuous and regular information exchange with local decision-makers could be established. Through such systematic feedback, actual needs could be evaluated in a meaningful and useful way. It must be remembered, however, that obtaining direct feedback from politicians is always a long and difficult process. Furthermore, politicians often expect miracles from evaluation and, given its known limits, all those in the field should try to meet the policy-makers' needs in terms of the presentation of the evaluation results, their accessibility and the politicians' major concerns about their policy measures, but also be clear about what evaluation can provide and what it cannot.

The drugs issue is a highly individual one. A policy aimed at people cannot, and should not, be guided purely by arithmetic or statistics. Many factors are at play which determine the success or failure of a drugs policy, and not all social processes

([44]) For more details of the EDDRA information system, see Chapters 11 and 12.

can be evaluated or controlled by policies. The same basic rule can apply to research as to a policy: it should be continuously subject to examination and improvements by methods other than purely scientific ones. Yet, on one point, at any rate, evaluation and politics have something in common: sometimes something just works, and no one knows why.

References

European Monitoring Centre for Drugs and Drug Addiction (1999), *Annual report on the state of the drugs problem in the European Union 1999,* Lisbon, EMCDDA.

European Monitoring Centre for Drugs and Drug Addiction (1998), *Annual report on the state of the drugs problem in the European Union 1998,* Lisbon, EMCDDA.

European Monitoring Centre for Drugs and Drug Addiction (1997), *Annual report on the state of the drugs problem in the European Union 1997,* Lisbon, EMCDDA.

European Monitoring Centre for Drugs and Drug Addiction (1995), *Annual report on the state of the drugs problem in the European Union 1995,* Lisbon, EMCDDA.

CHAPTER 11

EDDRA: CREATING A EUROPEAN INFORMATION SYSTEM ON DRUG-DEMAND REDUCTION

Teresa Salvador-Llivina

Information needs in the field of drug-demand reduction

During the past decades, interest in health and well-being and how to create a more equitable and fairer society has grown in all European Union Member States. At the same time, many social problems have emerged at national, regional and local level as a result of recession, unemployment, social migration and deprivation, and other socio-economic factors. Evident among these social problems are those relating to drug abuse, and even while the prevalence of some drugs is declining or stabilising in most Member States, new substances are constantly entering the market and their consumption among some social groups is increasing. The limited achievements to date of drug policies based on supply reduction has led to an awareness of the need to improve the efficacy of demand-reduction strategies in Europe (Salvador-Llivina and Ware, 1995).

To reinforce substantially the field of drug-demand reduction, policy-makers, scientists, drug professionals and others involved in this area all need to increase their understanding of how demand-reduction interventions can help to alleviate current problems, as well as what constitutes good practice in the field (Alvarez-Vara, 1993). Up-to-date, high-quality information is required on how to implement effective programmes, how to establish indicators for success and how to develop good evaluation practice.

Responding to that need requires a tool capable of providing reliable information in the easiest, cheapest and quickest possible way to facilitate coordination and avoid duplication of effort (Salvador-Llivina, 1995). To create such a device, the European drug demand-reduction field must overcome the many obstacles to communication encountered in this multi-sectorial and complex area. In the context of the EU, this is not an easy task. Significant cultural diversities are found both among and within countries regarding the perception of drugs, ways of identifying the causes of drug-related problems and the measures used to deal with them. In addition, distinct demand-reduction policies, variations in the scientific and professional background of the actors involved and the variety of European languages spoken all render communication even more complex.

One of the main areas of competence of the European Monitoring Centre for Drugs and Drug Addiction (EMCDDA) is drug-demand reduction. The EMCDDA aims to improve both the quality and the accessibility of information on demand-reduction interventions in Europe by collecting and analysing existing data, improving data-comparison methods and disseminating relevant information ([45]).

The establishment of a European information system on drug demand-reduction interventions was one of the priorities of the EMCDDA's first three-year work programme (1995 to 1997). This information system was to be based on a set of principles regarding information collection, interpretation and dissemination (Orthne and Blum, 1989; Buckland, 1991; Avgerou and Cornford, 1993; Anderson and Aydin, 1997; Heathfield et al., 1997; Carise et al., 1999), and the Centro de Estudios sobre la Promoción de la Salud (CEPS), Madrid, was contracted to create and test a prototype system.

Initial aim of the system

The main aim of the information system, now known as the Exchange on drug demand-reduction action (EDDRA), was to respond to the different information needs of scientists, policy-makers, decision-makers and practitioners involved in planning and implementing demand-reduction activities in Europe. This goal had to be reached by identifying, collecting and disseminating objective and comparable information. Closely related to this, the system had to integrate both the latest technological tools for collecting, storing and disseminating data, and high-quality standards regarding the content of the information gathered (Meyer et al., 1996; Johnson, 1997).

These two elements — latest technology and quality standards — were considered essential components of an information tool that would provide the services currently lacking in the European drug demand-reduction field. Furthermore, the system had to be cost-effective and user-friendly both for those entering data and for those searching for information.

Mapping existing needs

The preliminary steps in creating the system included identifying information sources, defining potential users and assessing their information needs in all the EU Member States through a detailed analysis of:

- the national reports on drug demand-reduction activities prepared by each national reference centre of the European Prevention Assessment System (EPAS, 1994) ([46]);

([45]) The EMCDDA's mandate is set out in Council Regulation (EEC) No 302/93 of 8 February 1993 (OJ L 36, 12.2.1993).

([46]) The EPAS project was funded by the European Commission to map the European drug-prevention field for the first time.

- the information maps and national reports prepared by the Reitox national focal points for the EMCDDA ([47]);
- a report on demand-reduction activities in Europe prepared for the EMCDDA (Nilson, 1995);
- a study of governmental and professional sources from each EU Member State (CEPS, 1995);
- a review of drug demand-reduction research in existing bibliographic repertories such as:
  - *Index Medicus* (descriptors: substance abuse; health promotion; health services; school health services);
  - *Excerpta Medica* (descriptors: public health; social medicine and hygiene; drug dependence; alcohol abuse; health policy and management; occupational health; industrial medicine);
  - *Current Contents* (descriptors: social and behavioural sciences; life sciences; clinical practice).

The data gathered from these sources not only provided a very realistic picture of the current status of drug-demand reduction in Europe, but also identified the obstacles to be overcome when establishing an instrument for data collection and dissemination in the field. The main problem areas included:

- the qualitative nature of most of the information available;
- the great heterogeneity of approaches reflecting cultural, political, professional and semantic differences across the EU;
- lack of an established evaluation culture in the field;
- lack of previously established national information systems to monitor drug demand-reduction interventions in most EU States;
- the long time delay between the end of a research project and the publication of its findings in the scientific literature;
- the added difficulty posed by the use of more than 11 languages at implementation.

Objectives of the EDDRA system

Both the information needs and the obstacles identified above had to be addressed in establishing the EDDRA system. Within this framework, its primary objectives were identified as follows:

- to provide reliable and comparable information on high-quality and scientifically backed demand-reduction interventions in the EU;
- to provide continuous, periodic and up-to-date information on ongoing programmes, especially innovative and collaborative projects;

([47]) An information map is an instrument devised by the EMCDDA to record in a uniform way the sources, availability, quality and flow of information in the EU Member States. National reports on the drug situation in each Member State are provided annually to the EMCDDA by the national focal points.

- to provide regular information on methods of implementing demand-reduction programmes;
- to provide information regarding evaluation, such as the outcomes of different demand-reduction approaches, results of interventions and their impact.

The secondary objectives of EDDRA were:

- to facilitate contact between professionals and teams who could benefit from each other's experience in diverse cultural settings;
- to create an educational tool capable of helping practitioners and teams to plan and report their project logically;
- to promote and facilitate both external and internal programme-evaluation information;
- to coordinate efforts with other European or international initiatives to profit from each other's work and avoid duplication of effort;
- to increase the visibility of the EMCDDA and its national focal points among drug demand-reduction professionals.

The feasibility study: developing and testing the prototype

Objectives of the feasibility study

The main objectives of the feasibility study, carried out in 1996 to 1997, were:

- to develop a tool designed to respond to existing needs;
- to confront and help to overcome current constraints;
- to test and fine-tune the prototype.

Methodology

The feasibility study was developed using interactive methodology with the involvement of the EMCDDA, CEPS as the coordinating body, the SEMA Group as the company responsible for creating the system's electronic architecture and the Reitox national focal points. Following the results of the initial review of sources described above, a preliminary proposal for a prototype was drawn up by CEPS, with input from the other actors involved. A coordination committee of representatives of the participating organisations was established to monitor the development of the feasibility study. The committee's tasks were to:

- coordinate aspects related to the system's implementation;
- introduce the use of EDDRA in each participating country;
- establish the work schedule;
- identify possible problems and ways of coping with them.

Several meetings were held during this period to review and discuss developments.

Once the prototype was ready, the feasibility study developed in three phases:

- testing the prototype in a limited number of countries;
- creating the final tools and producing the final outputs;
- implementing the system in all EU Member States.

Before testing began, several preparatory tasks were undertaken. These included defining the quality criteria demand-reduction programmes had to meet in order to be included in the system, completing the final paper and electronic questionnaires to be used to collect information on the programmes, and identifying which national focal points would participate in testing the prototype. The participating focal points were those of Belgium, Greece, the Netherlands and Sweden.

Defining quality criteria

To be eligible for inclusion, the demand-reduction projects had to demonstrate an evaluation component. In addition, quality criteria were established at the start of the feasibility phase for each participating focal point to follow in selecting initiatives for inclusion in EDDRA to ensure the accuracy of the information available via the system. The quality criteria were:

- programme identification (the organisation and contact person, centre or department responsible);
- type of programme approach;
- initial situation (the drug-related problems the project aimed to address);
- objectives of the intervention (general and specific);
- basic assumptions or theoretical foundation for the initiative;
- target population;
- status of the target population in relation to illegal drugs;
- substances addressed by the programme;
- programme setting;
- direct expected coverage;
- programme actions;
- number of staff or volunteers involved;
- geographical coverage;
- calendar;
- status of programme in relation to evaluation;
- total or annual programme budget;
- source of funding;
- programme abstract.

To ensure that each programme accepted for inclusion fulfilled the quality criteria, a set of attributes, validation rules and integrity constraints were defined for each database field. If the system detected no information in a field defined as a quality criterion, it would reject the project. Furthermore, coherence between stated objectives, plans for evaluation and the results presented was also established as a requirement.

The questionnaire

The questionnaire to be completed for each programme had to fulfil the following criteria:

- be comprehensive while still being concise;
- be straightforward, or at least not too time-consuming, to complete;
- be able to collect as much objective information as possible;
- allow projects to be compared;
- facilitate quick and easy access to information;
- provide different options for retrieving the information;
- facilitate different types of analysis of the information gathered.

Objectives during the testing phase

In September 1996, testing of the prototype began. The primary objectives were:

- to test the system's technical and technological structure and functioning;
- to test its capacity to produce objective, reliable and comparable information;
- to ensure its smooth and uniform functioning in the participating countries;
- to produce the first outcomes.

To meet these objectives, a comprehensive operational structure had to be defined and established. The operational goals for this trial period were to:

- establish the role of all participants (the EMCDDA, the CEPS coordinating team, the participating focal points and the SEMA Group);
- produce a pilot version of the information-collection questionnaire;
- set up an advisory committee to assess information needs and monitor the test phase;
- agree on the definitive name for the system;
- test and adopt the quality criteria;
- clearly define both the procedures and actors involved in standardising the information-collection process;
- produce the first outcomes of the system as both an electronic database and a paper manual;
- produce a final report summarising the implementation, results, obstacles encountered and proposals made to overcome them.

Outputs of the feasibility study

The feasibility study resulted in the following outputs:

- the EDDRA questionnaire, including eight main areas of information, together with an operational list of terms produced to facilitate comparability;

- guidelines to help the national focal points select projects for inclusion, including quality criteria, operational definitions of key demand-reduction terms and specific advice on how to enter projects into the database;
- the EDDRA users' manual containing a complete glossary of terms used and practical examples of how to complete each item of the questionnaire;
- an Internet newsgroup to promote the exchange of ideas, problem solving and so on, particularly regarding viewing projects in the database, modifying and improving the system's different applications, and identifying problems or bugs;
- on-site training seminars at each national focal point to discuss aspects of the practical implementation of the system such as:
  - using the different components;
  - navigating through the database;
  - applying the quality criteria;
  - entering projects into the database;
  - entering messages into the newsgroup;
  - elaborating strategies to promote the system;
  - deciding on the most suitable method of national information collection and dissemination;
- entering programmes in the database.

During the feasibility study, the focal points were required to search, select and produce information from a least five demand-reduction projects in their country (including treatment, drug-prevention and/or harm-reduction interventions). By the end of this period, 112 interventions had been entered, and suggestions to improve the electronic questionnaire registered.

Recommendations from the feasibility study

By the end of the feasibility study, EDDRA had proved to be a valuable instrument. It was able to produce objective, reliable and comparable information on drug demand-reduction activities in Europe, along with standards to promote good and evaluated practice in the field.

During this phase, the following recommendations were made to improve the functioning of the system.

Content

- The national EDDRA managers should be constantly and widely promoting and disseminating the quality criteria for inclusion in EDDRA.
- The questionnaire and operational definitions of key terms should be constantly fine-tuned during the first years of EDDRA's implementation at European level.

Technical aspects

- Technical aspects, such as reducing the time taken to upload, download and save data, must be adequately supported to avoid discouragement and the loss of working time by the focal points.
- A full-time professional must be appointed to provide constant technical assistance, at least for the first years of implementation.

Organisation

- The person appointed within each focal point to enter the programme information into the database should be fully trained in the main characteristics of EDDRA, and at the same time should have adequate knowledge and understanding of drug demand-reduction interventions in their own country.
- Broad participation should be encouraged, possibly by developing specific promotion strategies.
- As a key communication tool within the EDDRA project, the newsgroup should be continued during the general implementation phase.
- EDDRA should facilitate as far as possible broad access to information in each country. Creating a multilingual approach would substantially contribute to this aim.

Quality control and standardisation

- Due to the uneven quality of the projects entered by the national focal points, systematic screening should be undertaken centrally by the EMCDDA to ensure a basic level of quality and standardisation.
- The EMCDDA should undertake the centralised editing of the English of the project descriptions entered into the database.

Conclusions

The EDDRA information system has now grown, both in terms of its size and the experience gained by the parties involved, to 'adulthood' (48). Both positive and negative aspects identified by the participants in the feasibility phase have already been addressed by the EMCDDA and the EDDRA national managers based at the Reitox national focal points. As a next step, full participation in the EDDRA system by drug professionals from all EU Member States will help to stimulate and further enhance the quality of demand-reduction interventions in Europe.

(48) The current status of the EDDRA system is discussed in Chapter 12.

References

Alvarez-Vara, C. (1993), 'Evaluation: a challenge for the 90s', *COPE. EPAS Bulletin,* No 1, pp. 9–10.

Anderson, J. G., Aydin, C. E. (1997), 'Evaluating the impact of health care information systems', *International Journal for the Technological Assessment of Health Care,* No 21, pp. 380–93.

Avgerou, C., Cornford, T. (1993), *Developing information systems. Concepts, issues and practice,* London, Macmillan.

Buckland, M. (1991), *Information and information systems,* Westport, CT, Greenwood Press.

Carise, D., McLellan, A. T., Gifford, L. S., Kleber, H. D. (1999), 'Developing a national addiction treatment information system. An introduction to the Drug Evaluation Network System', *Journal of Substance Abuse Treatment,* No 21, pp. 67–77.

Centro de Estudios sobre la Promoción de la Salud (1995), 'Comparative study on drug abuse prevention policies of the Member States of the European Union', unpublished paper.

European Prevention Assessment System (1994), *European directory on drug demand reduction,* Madrid, CEPS.

Heathfield, H. A., Peel, V., Hudson, P., Kay, S., Mackay, L., Marley, T., Nicholson, L., Roberts, R., Williams, J. (1997), 'Evaluating large-scale health information systems: from practice towards theory', *Proceedings of the American Medical Informatics Association Annual Fall Symposium,* No 21, pp. 116–20.

Johnson, R. J. (1997), 'The development of a computerized health information system to facilitate program planning/evaluation and enhanced First Nations control of community health services', *Canadian Journal of Public Health,* No 21, pp. 207–9.

Meyer, K. E., Sather-Levine, B., Laurent-Bopp, D., Gruenewald, D., Nichol, P., Kimmerle, M. (1996), 'The impact of clinical information systems research on the future of advanced practice nursing', *Advanced Practice Nursing Quarterly,* No 21, pp. 58–64.

Nilson, M. (1995), 'Report on demand-reduction activities in Europe', unpublished report prepared for the EMCDDA.

Orthne, H. F., Blum, B. (Eds) (1989), *Implementing health care information systems,* New York, Springer-Verlag.

Salvador-Llivina, T. (1995), 'Technical information system on drug demand reduction: evaluation after six years of operation', in *International Congress on the Occasion of the European Drug Prevention Week 1994,* Cologne.

Salvador-Llivina, T., Ware, S. R. (1995), 'Drug abuse prevention policies and research in Europe: notes for a future agenda', *Drugs Education, Prevention and Policy,* No 2, pp. 7–15.

CHAPTER 12

EDDRA: CURRENT ACHIEVEMENTS AND FUTURE CHALLENGES

Philippe Roux

The advent of new technology, in particular the Internet, has heralded a new era in the dissemination and exchange of information, and the consequences of this information revolution have yet to be fully assessed. This is particularly true of information on drugs and drug addiction. From its creation in 1993, the European Monitoring Centre for Drugs and Drug Addiction (EMCDDA) has committed itself to making full use of the Internet and other new technologies to disseminate the information it gathers and analyses on drug use and its consequences. In this context, the EMCDDA not only developed an electronic network — the European information network on drugs and drug addiction or Reitox — linking its key partners in each of the EU Member States and the European Commission, but has also created a public website providing information on all aspects of the Centre's activities, products and services, with access to specialised databases and links to drug-information centres at national, European and international level ([49]).

It was within this context of technological innovation that the Centre developed its on-line information system, the Exchange on drug demand-reduction action (EDDRA) ([50]). The primary aim of the EDDRA system was to make publicly accessible detailed information on the various measures implemented in the 15 EU Member States to reduce the demand for drugs. The unique aspect of EDDRA is that it includes only those demand-reduction initiatives that have an evaluation component.

From the outset, the project posed both a technical and a scientific challenge. The technical challenge was to devise a tool that would allow the greatest exchange of information between the partners involved, and to create a multilingual database to permit the quickest, simplest and most efficient navigation by the general public. The scientific challenge was to find a standard way of collecting data that are difficult to access in the various Member States.

The context

Before discussing EDDRA in detail, it is important to mention the context in which it was created and the significance of the EMCDDA in this framework. The EMCDDA

([49]) The EMCDDA website is available at (http://www.emcdda.org).

([50]) The EDDRA information system is available at (http://www.emcdda.org/databases/databases_eddra.shtml).

was established in 1993 to improve knowledge about drugs and drug addiction in the EU in an attempt to combat the phenomenon.

As a major aspect of its mandate [51], reducing the demand for drugs occupies an important position among the six priorities of the EMCDDA's work programme for 1998 to 2000. These six priorities are:

- consolidating and improving information systems in the areas of epidemiology and demand reduction;
- consolidating and enhancing the Reitox network;
- improving and developing key indicators, methods and evaluation tools;
- improving the quality of the *Annual report on the state of the drugs problem in the European Union* (EMCDDA, 1995, 1997, 1998, 1999), the visibility of the work of the EMCDDA and the Reitox network and the dissemination of the information collected and produced by the Centre;
- developing cooperation with international partners, and ensuring synergy with the European Community action programme for the prevention of drug dependence [52];
- developing methodologies and tools to facilitate the comparison of the initiatives, laws, strategies and policies pursued by the different EU Member States.

The EMCDDA's efforts to reduce the demand for drugs, combined with those of its Reitox partners, focus on four main strategies:

- defining terminology to facilitate information exchange at EU level;
- promoting a culture of evaluation in Europe and making available relevant tools and guidelines to those working in the field;
- providing a chapter on demand reduction in the EMCDDA's *Annual report on the state of the drugs problem in the European Union*;
- developing the EDDRA information system, as well as other specialised databases and information media.

EDDRA: current status

The EDDRA database emerged from a simple premise: drug-prevention professionals are more inclined to include evaluation in their project designs when they are provided with concrete examples.

The EDDRA system currently comprises:

- an EU-wide network of national managers based at the Reitox national focal points;
- a standardised information-gathering tool in the form of a questionnaire;
- specially created software for editing the data collected off-line;
- a fully searchable database accessible via the EMCDDA website.

---

[51] See footnote 45.
[52] See footnote 7.

In order to reach as wide an audience as possible, a structure to permit the multilingual consultation of the database was developed for the 2000 version of the system. To date, texts are available in German, English and French and entries in all 11 official Community languages will be available by the end of 2000. It should be noted, however, that for obvious budgetary reasons some data are only available in the original language and in English.

Gathering the information

The EDDRA national managers form the core of the system. Their task is to gather data on national demand-reduction programmes that fulfil the single criterion of including a well-documented evaluation component.

While the national managers are the mainstay of the system, its cornerstone is the standardised questionnaire used to collect relevant information on the individual programmes. Accompanied by a comprehensive glossary of terms, the questionnaire divides the project information into nine sections:

- identification of the programme and its actors;
- the programme's background and objectives;
- its main characteristics;
- evaluation of the programme;
- the results of the evaluation;
- the programme budget;
- a programme abstract;
- the project outputs;
- specific comments.

The questionnaire contains a total of 48 questions, 11 of which have open fields to allow the national managers to describe the project in detail.

The information flow among the parties involved in the project is managed via a multilingual editing and messaging software created especially for EDDRA. This software allows the questionnaire to be edited off-line by the national managers and the files to be sent directly to the European manager at the EMCDDA by e-mail.

The information circuit can be summarised as follows:

- first, each national manager gathers relevant data on demand-reduction initiatives in their country via the EDDRA questionnaire, analyses them, edits them and sends the edited file via e-mail to the European manager at the EMCDDA;
- second, the European manager re-reads the questionnaires to ensure that all is complete and comprehensible before forwarding the entries to the Translation Centre for the Bodies of the European Union in Luxembourg for a final linguistic polishing;
- third, the European manager enters the final product into the database where it becomes accessible to the general public on-line.

This lengthy process is designed to ensure that the information contained in the EDDRA system is of the highest possible quality and accuracy. In this context, co-ordination meetings are regularly organised for all the partners involved to ensure the overall coherence of the project.

Searching the database

The database includes two search engines that permit:

- a rapid search by pre-defined fields, for example by country, programme approach, action or target group;
- an advanced search with eight separate fields that can be combined according to the user's needs, thus permitting, for example, a search for all evaluated projects in France that target heroin users.

Once the search has been submitted, the system provides a list of projects that meet the selected criterion or criteria together with accompanying abstracts and details of the relevant contact person. The user may view or download the complete project description which is presented in a standardised format to facilitate comparison between projects.

Technical challenges

Given the remarkable speed at which information technology is developing, no sooner has a computer product been installed than it is already obsolete. Managing a project that includes a complex information-technology component is, therefore, not an easy task, and even less so when the project involves partners throughout the 15 EU Member States with varying degrees of mastery of the technologies concerned.

Where information technology is concerned, there are always several alternative possibilities at any one time, each with its own advantages and limitations, and 'compromise' is thus the key word. What is required is a product that can be easily updated and adapted to changing technologies and that can be used by the widest possible audience. For databases accessed via the Internet, response time is a crucial element and the interface and search tools must therefore be designed to ensure the swiftest possible handling of the user's request. As a result, when developing these tools a compromise must be reached between efficiency and precision.

Scientific challenges

EDDRA's aim to provide information only on European drug demand-reduction projects that include an evaluation component also poses a twofold scientific challenge.

The first difficulty concerns the fact that EDDRA was devised to encourage the development of an evaluation culture in Europe. Since evaluation is virtually unknown in the field of drug prevention, very few drug demand-reduction initiatives in Europe have to date been effectively assessed. It is thus a considerable challenge to gather and disseminate information that does not actually exist. Yet, rather than creating deadlock, this potential contradiction is in fact a strong point of the system.

EDDRA is much more than 'just another database'. Instead, it is the tool of an extremely ambitious project to support the development of a real evaluation culture in the 15 Member States — hence the criterion that all projects in the system must include an evaluation component. Yet this evaluation does not have to be complete for the project to be incorporated into the system. Including projects in EDDRA is a way of 'rewarding' the teams involved for their efforts to evaluate their actions and a means of encouraging them to continue doing so. For this incentive-based approach to succeed, the EMCDDA and its partners must ensure that the EDDRA system is made widely known at EU level, and the national managers are currently exploring ways of actively promoting EDDRA.

In any event, a balance must also be struck between the quality and quantity of the projects in the database. EDDRA can be seen, to some degree, as an indicator by which to observe and quantify the evolution of a European evaluation culture. The system currently contains about 100 demand-reduction projects, encompassing different approaches and responses to drug addiction, which more or less satisfy the fundamental eligibility criterion. This figure is expected to increase fourfold by the end of 2000.

The second scientific challenge relates to the actual editing of the contents. While it is undoubtedly of real interest to professionals in the field to share their knowledge on an EU-wide scale, reporting skills are sorely lacking. A large part of the national managers' work thus consists of helping local teams to edit and present their projects effectively. Despite such assistance in completing the questionnaire, a large number of project descriptions remain incomplete, thus creating a lack of homogeneity among them notwithstanding the attempts at standardisation described above.

The EMCDDA is supporting the efforts of the national EDDRA managers by organising joint training schemes with the Reitox national focal points focusing on improving the reporting and evaluation skills of EU demand-reduction professionals. These efforts will be continued in 2000, but still remain insufficient given the few financial resources available and the extent of the task.

Conclusions

Report-writing skills are an essential component of activities in the fields of social work and public health. They are the starting point for all evaluation protocols and processes to improve working practices. Enhancing the quality of these reports is currently the most crucial task facing the national EDDRA managers. This issue should receive wider recognition and has implications for the topics covered by both initial and continuing training courses for social-work and health professionals.

The national EDDRA managers and the EMCDDA have to date dedicated significant efforts to improving the quality of the data provided by the system. In addition, in order better to meet the needs of those working in the field, considerable work has been undertaken to facilitate their access to the different resources and materials available via the system. These efforts include:

- making the EDDRA manuals available in all 11 Community languages;
- supplying the national managers with a multilingual version of the EDDRA editing and messaging software;
- restructuring the database to allow navigation in all Community languages (to be achieved by the end of 2000) and access to the individual project data in the original language and in English.

In spite of major budgetary restrictions, the EMCDDA is investigating the possibility of making the EDDRA database entirely multilingual. All these efforts form a significant part of the EMCDDA's contribution to the development of an evaluation culture in the field of drug-demand reduction in Europe.

References

European Monitoring Centre for Drugs and Drug Addiction (1999), *Annual report on the state of the drugs problem in the European Union 1999*, Lisbon, EMCDDA.

European Monitoring Centre for Drugs and Drug Addiction (1998), *Annual report on the state of the drugs problem in the European Union 1998*, Lisbon, EMCDDA.

European Monitoring Centre for Drugs and Drug Addiction (1997), *Annual report on the state of the drugs problem in the European Union 1997*, Lisbon, EMCDDA.

European Monitoring Centre for Drugs and Drug Addiction (1995), *Annual report on the state of the drugs problem in the European Union 1995*, Lisbon, EMCDDA.

CHAPTER 13

PROMOTING EVALUATION AND ENHANCING SKILLS

Sabine Haas

Since 1997, the Österreichisches Bundesinstitut für Gesundheitswesen (Austrian Health Institute — ÖBIG) has been actively promoting evaluation, both in its capacity as the Reitox national focal point for Austria and as national coordinating body for European Drug Prevention Week (EDPW) 1998. This experience has revealed both the rapidly growing interest in evaluation in Europe — as increasingly reflected in practical activities — and major deficiencies in the basic knowledge, skills, framework and conditions required for good evaluation practice.

These deficits are not surprising, given that although evaluation is a scientific concept, it is primarily local practitioners and politicians who are involved in planning and implementing measures designed to reduce the demand for drugs. For a long time, these groups did not consider evaluation to be a necessary element of demand-reduction programmes and, with limited funding available, adding a 'scientific' component was regarded as a 'luxury' and not a priority for limited resources which would be better spent on working directly with the target group. Moreover, evaluation has often been seen as a task that could not be carried out effectively with the skills available within the project.

On the other hand, there has been an increasing demand for evaluation as an 'objective assessment of success' over the past few years. At the same time, interest in, and awareness of the need to acquire, the necessary skills have also grown. In considering the issue of disseminating the knowledge and abilities required for evaluation, at least three questions arise.

- Who are the target groups?
- What knowledge should be conveyed as a matter of priority?
- How can this be done?

Reaching the target groups: top down and bottom up

A distinction should be made between at least two relevant target groups and, on the basis of these groups, two different approaches to promoting evaluation. The 'top-down' approach is geared to decision-makers and funding bodies and attempts to convince them of the importance of evaluation. This is relevant for improving the framework conditions for evaluation. While evaluation often still fails because of inadequate resources, it can also be promoted and motivated by means of financial guidelines. This is illustrated, for example, by the fact that many Austrian facilities providing help for drug addicts have become involved in evaluation for the first time in the context of EU programmes, such as the Community action programme for the prevention of drug dependence [53], and have 'acquired a taste for it' in the process.

Although the top-down approach must not be neglected, this chapter focuses above all on the 'bottom-up' approach. This is targeted at drug-prevention experts active at local level and attempts to convey to them that evaluation is both meaningful and useful. A secondary aim is to motivate them to evaluate their own projects and to learn in the process. This method should therefore be directed at the largest possible number of drug demand-reduction practitioners, and not simply at a restricted group of those working explicitly on evaluation, scientific reporting or project planning.

For a variety of reasons, it is both necessary and worthwhile to convey background knowledge and promote a better understanding of evaluation among the widest possible group of drug practitioners. As the process becomes more comprehensible and better understood, so the uneasiness that is frequently felt about external evaluation is reduced. Promoting an understanding of the concept can also increase the level of identification with all forms of assessment and its results as well as reducing the level of inhibition about initiating an internal evaluation and about ongoing involvement with it.

Whether internal or external, evaluations require support and input from a number of parties active in the specific project or programme who are often also involved in generating the evaluation tools. This input may include documenting current work and experience or generating questionnaires and tests. The quality of an evaluation usually depends on the reliability of the data and information obtained at grass-roots level. The best way of ensuring this quality is for everybody involved to understand that this 'additional' work is both meaningful and necessary.

Defining objectives, presenting projects and planning evaluation

ÖBIG's experience, both of analysing the national projects for inclusion in the Exchange on drug demand-reduction action (EDDRA) database and as national coordinating body for the EDPW 1998, is that, even with the necessary motivation, implementing evaluation still raises a number of problems.

One fundamental issue — which became apparent both in the context of the EDDRA system and in project applications for EDPW 1998 — is defining objectives and the basic assumptions underlying them. Project managers often have difficulty presenting the principles behind their activities in a pre-set, standardised format. Nor is it easy to distinguish between the objectives and basic assumptions of a project and the methods applied. This probably reflects the different logic of practice-

[53] See footnote 7.

oriented and scientifically oriented project planning. Measures designed to reduce the demand for drugs are often planned and conceived on the basis of aspects other than those required for a 'scientific' presentation. For example, projects evolve according to changing political priorities or deficits detected during practical work. In this context, the goals pursued are not always specifically and 'scientifically' recorded and are rarely operationalised.

An associated and inter-linked problem lies in making the implicit elements of a project explicit, both for the project managers themselves and, in due course, for others. Regarding EDDRA, it often becomes clear from the material available or from personal discussions that activities are more varied, more extensive and more soundly based than is apparent from the questionnaire completed by the project managers. The everyday reality of the project often leads those closely involved to take major aspects of it for granted and to lose sight of the fact that these same aspects are fundamental. As a result, they are omitted from the project description. If the project managers work together to complete or revise the questionnaire, this can be an eye-opener for them too, shedding new light on their own perception of their project.

Not only do these problems in designing and presenting programmes make it difficult to describe them consistently and comprehensibly — as required not only by EDDRA, for example, but also increasingly by other project applications, such as the Community action programme at EU level or the 'Healthy Austria Fund' at national level — they also create obstacles to evaluation. A clear definition of the objectives and basic assumptions (both practical and theoretical) involved in a programme is essential if goals are to be expressed in operational terms and methods and tools developed to review their achievement. However, if these aims remain either un- or ill-defined it becomes more difficult to plan the evaluation, and planning is both one of the most important and one of the most difficult stages of any assessment. While it is often not easy to define the methods, tools and indicators by which experiences and 'successes' can both be evaluated and implemented in practice, this is crucial to ensure the quality and usefulness of the data and information obtained. If the project objectives are made clear from the outset, the evaluation will be easier to plan.

Methods and tools: materials, training

Experience in Austria to date indicates that evaluation skills must be conveyed in a manner that is as specific and practice-oriented as possible. This was apparent, for example, from the first announcements of the EDDRA database in the newsletter *DrugNet Austria* (ÖBIG, 1997), which were fairly theoretical and elicited no response. Only when the published abstracts of the EDDRA projects were very specific, clear and practice-oriented were interest and demand triggered. When the methods and results were described, the evaluation required also became less frightening, as these aspects showed, for example, how an evaluation can be carried out and what the results can be. This, in turn, often sounded practice-oriented, clear and comprehensible, rather than scientifically complex.

While providing guidelines and manuals is an important form of support for evaluation work, it is not sufficient as these materials do not facilitate individual discussion of specific problems and interaction is limited, even when there is good educational preparation. However, these tools can represent an important addition to advanced training interventions, which themselves constitute an appropriate first step towards conveying the relevant knowledge. ÖBIG offered its first training measures for Austrian drug-prevention professionals in October 1999. Based on the need for advanced training and knowledge transfer described above, these seminars focused on project presentation on the one hand — in particular, defining objectives and fundamental assumptions based on the EDDRA questionnaire — and basic information on evaluation — operationalising objectives, defining possible indicators and tools, and so on — on the other. Participation in the one-day events was free.

The training offered was geared primarily to drug practitioners either marginally involved in evaluation, dealing with evaluation in their everyday working lives, or merely interested in the topic. In terms of methodology, it was attempted to gear the training to practice by working with specific case studies provided or suggested by the participants. A major part of the training consisted of teamwork, which promoted the independent application of what had been learned and facilitated a flexible response to the specific difficulties that arose. Using the EDDRA information-collection questionnaire and the EMCDDA *Guidelines for the evaluation of drug prevention* (EMCDDA, 1998) helped to bring these materials to life and hence to make them more easily applicable in practice.

The experience gained during the training events was positive. Austrian drug experts showed much greater interest than expected in the content and the feedback was very good. The participants themselves said that the seminars made them feel better prepared and more strongly motivated to work on evaluation. The training offered was perceived as a helpful and meaningful measure and further, more detailed training events — particularly with regard to information on evaluation — were requested. Follow-up training at a higher level will therefore be provided.

Learning by doing: quality circles, helpdesk, peer exchange

In the long term, however, training will only be effective if it is put into practice. Learning by doing is the most exciting and also the most sustained way of acquiring knowledge and experience. However, in the field of drug demand reduction, this process has not as yet been adequately supported by the expertise and knowledge available.

At the end of 1999, therefore, as a follow-up to the training seminars mentioned above, ÖBIG arranged for a 'quality circle' on evaluation to be established in the Vienna area. The idea was to improve the quality of evaluation practice by providing a forum for discussing specific plans and evaluation projects, and for exchanging knowledge relating to theoretical and methodological issues. In this way the circle would support the principle of 'learning by doing'. For example, at the first meetings, participants discussed the methodological problems of evaluating drug-prevention measures on the basis of a specific project and general questions relating to process evaluation.

Drug experts involved in evaluation showed great interest in the idea and it was agreed that they would meet once a month for three hours to exchange relevant knowledge and experience. In addition to practitioners working in local drug facilities and projects, a number of scientific experts also attended the meetings. There was particular interest in discussing issues and problems arising from practical evaluation work (integration into the everyday life of a project, staff motivation, methodological options and limitations).

Conclusions

The regional activities described above should now be both supported and supplemented at European level. A 'helpdesk' based at the EMCDDA could offer support and advice on very specific issues and problems, suggest possible methods and tools for evaluation, and draw attention to existing experience. This could be of great assistance to those involved in planning and implementing evaluations at local level. It could also help to improve the quality of evaluations as the 'central' level would be more aware of the kinds of questions and problems people were facing when implementing evaluation at local level. In response, the materials, support and so on they provide to them could be improved accordingly.

A peer exchange would similarly stimulate the exchange of ideas and experience by experts involved or interested in evaluation, and would thus also support and promote a learning process. Furthermore, cooperation and information exchange extending beyond the individual project and, in particular, across national borders, could greatly increase motivation for undertaking evaluations. In organising a peer exchange of this kind, use could be made of the experiences and structures of the European networks already in existence in the drugs field, such as the Federation of European Professionals Working in the Field of Drug Abuse (ERIT) or the European Association of Professionals Working with Drug Dependencies (Itaca) ([54]).

References

European Monitoring Centre for Drugs and Drug Addiction (1998), *Guidelines for the evaluation of drug prevention*, Manuals No 1, Lisbon, EMCDDA.

ÖBIG (1997), *DrugNet Austria*, bimonthly newsletter of the Österreichisches Bundesinstitut für Gesundheitswesen, November/December.

([54]) Information on ERIT can be found at (http://www.erit.org) and on Itaca at (http://www.itaca-europe.org).

CHAPTER 14

THE CHALLENGE OF EVALUATION FOR LOCAL COMMUNITIES

Joana Judice

A large number of European towns, particularly those affected by 'drug tourism' and the organisation of major music festivals, 'rave' parties and other similar events, are questioning the relevance of drug-prevention messages aimed at children and teenagers ([55]). In fact, the emergence in recreational culture of new synthetic drugs such as ecstasy, use of which is increasingly prevalent among young people, has emphasised regional authorities' feeling of powerlessness in regard to drug prevention, especially since the prevention programmes established to date do not appear to have an effect on young people who do not identify with the traditional image of the drug addict these programmes promote.

In the context of the general task of drug prevention, for which local authorities are responsible, political decision-makers now acknowledge that it is vital to establish primary-prevention programmes aimed specifically at children and teenagers.

The growing popularity of synthetic 'dance' drugs among the young, and the increasing use of licit with illicit drugs at an early age, is now forcing a preventive response from local communities.

The challenge of evaluation for politicians

Evaluation can help policy-makers:

- decide whether an action should be implemented, changed or expanded;
- justify the funds allocated;
- interpret quantifiable data;
- validate the prevention methods used.

In addition, evaluating the effectiveness of primary drug prevention demonstrates the extent to which it has helped reduce the number of drug users as well as the health risks they face. This undertaking may seem impossible given the constantly

([55]) This chapter is based on the Réseau SécuCités-Drogues network project that examined the relevance of drug-prevention messages aimed at children, teenagers and vulnerable groups, particularly in response to the increasing use of new synthetic drugs (Réseau SécuCités-Drogues, 1999).

shifting drug scene, both in terms of the drugs supply and methods of drug use, an argument often put forward by those drug-prevention professionals who do not evaluate their programmes. This position is characteristic of the 'all-or-nothing' approach to drug prevention, because while it is difficult to evaluate the impact of drug prevention in general, it is nevertheless possible to evaluate specific programmes from different perspectives.

At the preliminary stage of the Réseau SécuCités-Drogues project, school drug-prevention and/or health-education measures that used different methods were identified in 15 European towns ([56]). Two of the resulting evaluations — one of a project targeting children in Barcelona, Spain, and the other of a project targeting teenagers in Saint-Herblain, France — are described below.

Evaluation of a drug-prevention project in Barcelona

Reasons for establishing a drug-prevention programme

In Barcelona, a city of 1 508 805 inhabitants, polydrug use is a major problem ([57]), affecting around 9 000 people. The most commonly used substances are alcohol, tobacco and tranquillisers, and alcoholism in particular is of great concern to local authorities and local politicians. Children are frequently confronted by the problem of drug addiction in their own environment and the need to establish an effective drug-prevention programme aimed at them was justified by a study on the prevalence of tobacco use among schoolchildren. In 1989, an intervention based on this study began to take shape.

Strategy used

The first stage was to create a partnership on prevention. The Institut Municipal de la Salut (Local Authority Institute of Public Health) proposed developing school drug-prevention programmes in collaboration with external parties, such as teachers and pupils, health services, associations including youth groups, and social services. These drug-prevention programmes would form part of a general health-education policy and be targeted at three main age groups: 8–11-year-olds; 11–13-year-olds; and those aged 13 and over. The second stage was to establish these programmes in schools.

The PASE programme

One such programme was the Programa de prevenció de l'abús de substàncies addictives (PASE), a medium-term (12 to 18 months) tobacco-, alcohol- and drug-prevention programme aimed at children aged 11 to 13. The project, devised by the

([56]) Mons (Belgium); Odense (Denmark); Hamburg, Karlsruhe and Munich (Germany); Barcelona (Spain); Argenteuil (France); Bologna and Milan (Italy); Vienna (Austria); Loures (Portugal); Belfast, Nottingham and Sheffield (UK); Oslo (Norway).

([57]) See footnote 23.

Institut Municipal de la Salut, is managed by the Departament de Promoció de la Salut (Health Promotion Department) and aims to reduce the incidence of tobacco addiction by 25 %, to reduce the consumption of alcoholic drinks (notably at weekends) by 25 % and to strengthen negative attitudes to substance abuse. A pilot programme was established during the 1989/90 school year which proved highly successful with both pupils and teachers. In 1996 to 1997, the programme was implemented in 63 state, 68 co-educational and 10 private schools involving 7 667 pupils.

The programme focuses on helping children to identify social pressures, to withstand advertising strategies and peer pressure, to acquire social skills and to clarify their own values and attitudes to the substances that cause dependence. While the basic work is geared to preventing smoking, emphasis is placed on the harmful effects of those substances with which children are familiar and the PASE programme also covers the consumption of alcohol and cannabis. The programme includes 10 activities — covering issues such as dependence and peer pressure — which are integrated into everyday classroom activities.

Evaluation

Evaluation of the PASE programme assessed both its activities and its effectiveness using an experimental group and a control group. The two groups attended an information session at the start of the programme to increase their awareness of both licit and illicit drugs, and the experimental group then followed the programme.

The evaluation results showed a difference in attitudes to tobacco among the two groups, with the control group more tolerant of tobacco advertising. These data were collected via:

- a questionnaire for teachers;
- a form for monitoring and evaluating activities completed by the teachers administering the programme;
- a questionnaire for pupils, distributed at the start of the programme, at the end of the school year and in the middle of the following school year.

Direct monitoring of the programme by the team that created it was also an important source of information, particularly for comparing the original outcome expectations with how the programme actually developed. However, this type of analysis is subjective and can only complement an external evaluation.

Obstacles to the programme

Evaluation found that the programme is more appropriate for the 11 to 12 age group. For those aged 12 to 13, it was recommended to use the Decidex ('You decide!') drug-prevention programme which combines different strategies, primarily focusing on enhancing the skills to decide whether or not to use drugs and relating drug use with adolescent lifestyles and problems.

In addition, lack of time was frequently mentioned as a problem for teachers, as was lack of resources for some schools and the teachers' impression that they were overloaded with work.

Evaluation of a drug-prevention project in Saint-Herblain

Reasons for establishing a drug-prevention programme

After several years of activities for preventing drug addiction, such as annual drug-information interventions in schools, the local authority of Saint-Herblain, a town of 43 689 inhabitants, was alerted in 1990 by a school head teacher that cannabis was being sold and used in the school.

Strategy used

The first stage in responding to this problem was to establish a local coalition on prevention. A pilot group, Prévention des toxicomanies (drug addiction prevention), brought together the various services concerned to develop a common drug-prevention strategy to be implemented in all schools. It was decided that the evaluation should be carried out externally by the Institut National de la Santé et de la Recherche Médicale (National Institute for Health and Medical Research — Inserm). The second stage was to establish the primary-prevention programme in schools.

The primary-prevention programme

The programme was devised by two local-authority departments, the Délégation Permanente de Prévention et de Sécurité Urbaine (Permanent Delegation for Prevention and Urban Security — DPPSU) and the Centre Communal de Promotion de la Santé (Health Promotion Community Centre — CCPS). Its aim was both to encourage pupils aged 11, 13 and 14 to behave responsibly when confronted with the problem of drug addiction, and to enable teachers to recognise signs of malaise among pupils before the symptoms of drug addiction actually appeared, to identify those in difficulty when faced with these problems and to know what attitude they should take. In 1992, the programme was implemented among 531 students in four schools.

The programme consists of:

- a health game (snakes and ladders) to make children aware of the effects of their behaviour on both their health and their environment (year 6 pupils — 11 years old);
- a drama forum, to challenge pupils about the risks associated with certain kinds of drug-related behaviour (year 4 pupils — 13 years old);
- a lecture by a health professional to inform pupils about the physiological and mental effects associated with drug-taking (year 3 pupils — 14 years old).

Evaluation

A team from Inserm evaluated the programme using an experimental group from Saint-Herblain and a control group from Rezé, a nearby town with a similar social structure to Saint-Herblain. The evaluation covered how the programme had been set up and its effects, and involved a quality and gender-based analysis according to the sex of the pupils.

The initial objectives were:

- to measure the differences between the two groups from the point of view of life-style and the perceived availability of alcohol, tobacco and drugs;
- to introduce preventive measures targeting young people as well as adults;
- to gauge young people's satisfaction with the programme activities, their attitude to drug prevention and their opinions and attitudes to alcohol, tobacco and drugs.

Year 3 pupils (aged 14 to 15) were questioned about whether or not they had been involved throughout the entire four-year programme. Two separate questionnaires were drawn up, one for the Saint-Herblain pupils and one for the Rezé pupils, and the experimental group also answered a few additional questions.

The evaluation results suggest that the PASE programme's drug-prevention measures changed perceptions to, as well as actual use of, the target substances. The young people from Saint-Herblain had a more definite opinion on drugs, were more aware of sales outlets for illicit drugs, used them less and intended to use cannabis less in the future than the pupils from Rezé. The evaluation also showed that those parties actively involved in the programme had the young people's trust.

Obstacles to the programme

Parental involvement in the programme was poor, and although most parents had been informed about it, only one in 12 actually attended. A large number, however, discussed the programme with their children at home.

The young people themselves appreciated the programme, but did not believe it was useful.

Conclusions

The following factors characterise good drug-prevention practice at local level.

- The decision to form a local partnership. The courts and the police may even need to be included so that the interventions established complement each other and that the role of all parties is clear, particularly to the target group, in this case young people.
- Creating an evaluation plan before starting the action.

- Evaluating the project according to a few, selected criteria. While evaluation is relative as regards the programme's long-term impact, it also allows the programmes to be adapted as necessary, generates concrete, scientific results and not simply assumptions based on observation, and contributes to a better understanding of the theory behind the programmes.
- Providing the necessary means, however modest, to achieve the objectives. Good practice allows communication about health promotion without focusing exclusively on the products targeted.

It remains difficult, however, to motivate decision-makers when evaluation results are not visible until a few years later. This is usually the result of insufficient funds being allocated by the local authority.

References

Réseau SécuCités-Drogues (1999), *La pertinence des messages de prévention. Projet 1998–99,* Paris, Forum Européen pour la Sécurité Urbaine.

Further reading

Becker-Textor, I., Schubert, E., Strick, R. (1997), *Ohne Spielzeug,* Herder.

Calafat, A. (1998), *Characteristics and social representation of ecstasy in Europe,* Valencia, Irefrea and the European Commission.

Choquet, M., Lagadic, C. (1997), *Evaluation en milieu scolaire d'un programme de prévention primaire en matière de toxicomanie,* Villejuif, Inserm.

Costes, J. M., Carpentier, C. (1996), *Drogues et toxicomanies — indicateurs et tendances,* Paris, Observatoire Français des Drogues et des Toxicomanies.

Domes, R., Rabes, M. (1997), *European model project compiled ecstasy material,* Hamburg, Büro für Suchtprävention.

European Commission (1998), *The European Union in action against drugs,* Luxembourg, Office for Official Publications of the European Communities.

European Commission (1997), *Resolution on the communication from the Commission to the Council and the European Parliament on the control of new synthetic drugs (designer drugs),* Brussels, European Commission.

European Monitoring Centre for Drugs and Drug Addiction (1998), *Guidelines for the evaluation of drug prevention,* Manuals No 1, Lisbon, EMCDDA.

European Monitoring Centre for Drugs and Drug Addiction (1997), *New trends in synthetic drugs in the European Union,* Insights No 1, Lisbon, EMCDDA.

Forum Européen pour la Sécurité Urbaine (1999), 'La Pertinence des messages de prévention — Notes de travail pour le Séminaire de Mons'.

Forum Européen pour la Sécurité Urbaine (1998), *Prévention des toxicomanies à l'école primaire*, Paris, Forum Européen pour la Sécurité Urbaine.

Lewis, R., Sherval, J. (1997), 'Demand reduction activities related to "new synthetic drugs": MDMA (ecstasy), other amphetamines and LSD in European Union Member States', Centre for HIV/AIDS and Drug Studies (CHADS), Edinburgh.

Observatoire Français des Drogues et des Toxicomanies (1998), *Consommation d'ecstasy en France: indicateurs et tendances*, Paris, OFDT.

Parquet, P. J. (1998), *Pour une prévention de l'usage des substances psychoactives — usage, usage nocif, dépendance*, Vanves, Editions CFES.

Springer, A., Uhl, A. (Eds) (1998), *Evaluation research in regard to primary prevention of drug abuse*, Brussels, European Commission.

Springer, A., Uhl, A. (Eds) (1995), 'Primärprävention des Drogenmissbraucs und ihre Evaluation', Untersuchung des Ludwig Boltzmann-Instituts für Suchtforschung im Auftrag des Bundesministeriums für Wissenschaft und Verkehr, Vienna.

Van der Stel, J. (Ed.) (1998), *Handbook prevention: alcohol, drugs and tobacco*, Strasbourg, Pompidou Group of the Council of Europe.

CHAPTER 15

THE LIMITS OF EVALUATION

Alfred Uhl

> *Green's Law: 'Anything is possible if you don't know what you're talking about!'* (Bloch, 1985)

Societies have always been confronted by the fact that individuals suffer from severe physical, psychical and social problems, and that these problems usually affect other individuals as well as society as a whole. Societies are responsible for taking appropriate measures to combat these problems, but in what specific areas? And what are 'appropriate measures'?

At first sight, the answers seem simple. Most people agree that interventions should begin before problems arise, that the emphasis should be on helping and convincing individuals rather than coercing them, that the private sphere of individuals and their basic rights should not be violated and that measures should be as effective and efficient as possible. In other words, the focus should be on primary prevention, educational approaches and evaluated measures, and decisions should be based on real scientific evidence.

Looking more closely, the situation is far more complex. While there are myriad problems to tackle, resources for drug prevention and evaluation are limited and priorities therefore have to be set. Very often, what is lacking is a sound empirical or theoretical basis on which to build strategic decisions. More specific research on prevention is clearly needed, but some very interesting and important research questions are beyond economic and/or epistemological feasibility. Those working in the drug-prevention field are often faced with phenomena that are hard to assess reliably, with a long latency period between intervention and outcome, low problem incidence, a large variety of uncontrollable simultaneous influences and important contextual factors that change rapidly over time and vary from region to region.

Currently, an increasing demand for drug prevention and evaluation can be observed throughout the European Union. This demand correlates with high expectations of the feasibility of prevention and evaluation. Many experts are fascinated by the growing practical importance of their fields, but feel uneasy about the equally growing gap between rising expectations and what can realistically be achieved.

This leads to a fundamental dilemma regarding how to proceed which can be expressed in terms of the following three problematic positions:

- anti-scientism;
- deliberate ignorance of methodology;
- cynical opportunism.

'Anti-scientism' is characterised by a rejection of quantitative science and basic research logic. This position is essentially irrational and fits nicely into contemporary alternative and esoteric trends. It is quite popular among those working in the practical field of drug prevention, who feel threatened by the demand to evaluate, who are not trained in the basic logic of research methodology and who are aware that many expensive evaluation projects do not produce conclusive evidence anyway. The proponents of anti-scientism claim to be in favour of 'process evaluation' and 'qualitative research', but what they aim at instead is a semantic trick to legitimise all forms of unsystematic and subjective data collection which are not suitable for assessing the value of certain approaches. It should be stressed that 'process evaluation' and 'qualitative research' — if properly defined and understood (see, for example, Uhl, 1998) — are central pillars of research and evaluation, and the present discussion is not intended to place these concepts in a negative light.

Proponents of the second position, 'deliberate ignorance of methodology', place great emphasis on experimental designs, inference statistics and objectivity, but they systematically avoid dealing with research limitations, statistical artefacts and methodology. They are commonly confronted with critics who reject their 'scientific' results based on practical experience and common sense. In this context, some researchers take the metaphorical expression 'blindness' as a synonym for 'scientific objectivity' far too literally.

'Cynical opportunism' characterises those researchers and evaluators who realise that much of what is produced as 'scientific evidence' is not conclusive at all, but who stick to common and widely accepted research strategies for pragmatic reasons because they simply do not know of a sensible alternative. In some ways, this understandable position comes close to fraud, but since virtually every critical researcher who has been working in the field for some time has to accept that some of his or her own published work might be classified in this category, even rigorous critics of the current state of research hesitate to apply such harsh labels. Is this cautious approach justified? Probably not. Researchers should not let inevitable mistakes of the past prevent them from naming problems explicitly and learning from them how to improve their work. If researchers resort uncritically to widely used fashions, repeat prevailing convictions, create the impression of being able to cope with any tasks, ignore fundamental uncertainties, deliberately misuse the ambiguity of terminology and neglect basic methodological problems, they can attract more customers for the time being, but in the long run risk losing the credibility of their profession.

There is definitely an alternative to these three positions. Research can and should represent an informed and critical effort to find lasting solutions to problems.

Expressing the inherent uncertainties encountered in daily drug-prevention and evaluation practice, highlighting weak spots, rejecting tasks that are not feasible because of economic and/or epistemological restraints, using precise terminology and facing up to methodological problems may risk disappointing potential customers, but will strengthen the profession and help to build a sound foundation for a good and lasting reputation.

Some practitioners in the field, frustrated by the complexity of the task and tempted by the need to tender for projects for economic reasons, may sympathise with one or other of the three problematic positions outlined above, but should rigorously reject them. Despite the difficulties encountered, there is room for optimism. Primary drug prevention and its evaluation are challenging tasks, but if the profession is really understood, despite all its limitations, numerous promising approaches, sensible options and solutions are available to prevent a lapse into depression or cynicism.

COST A-6: Evaluation of primary prevention in the field of illicit drugs

In 1992, the European Commission commissioned a project, Evaluation of action against drug abuse in Europe, within the framework of its Coopération Scientifique et Technologique (COST) to assess activities related to problems with illicit drugs ([58]).

At the initial project meeting, the task was split into five sub-tasks, each to be carried out by an independent working group. When the second working group (WG II), Evaluation of primary prevention in the field of illicit drugs, first met, two facts became immediately apparent:

- the list of properly evaluated primary drug-prevention projects in Europe was rather short;
- much more work was needed to base such projects on a sound theoretical basis.

WG II felt that the terminology used in drug prevention and evaluation was far too ambiguous and vague for a systematic discussion, and that some central methodological problems inherent to the field tended not to be adequately considered or analysed. As a result, a consensus study on definitions, concepts and problems was set up using the Delphi method developed by Dalkey and Helmer (1963) and popularised by Lindstone and Turoff (1975). Most concepts referred to in this chapter were developed in this study, and the final report (Uhl, 1998) is available free of charge at (http://www.api.or.at/lbisucht.htm).

Ambiguity of central terms and concepts

The inevitable ambiguity and vagueness of language can be — and is commonly and regularly — used as a powerful tool to mislead others without deceiving them

([58]) For more information on COST A-6, see (http://www.infoset.ch/inst/costa6/).

directly, and to circumvent insoluble problems by reinterpreting central terms. A rational, consistent and honest dialogue requires precise and unequivocal terminology. It does not matter whether words have different meanings as long as all parties are aware of this and can state precisely which meaning they are using. Logic dictates that definitions are conventions and cannot be true or false. Individuals cannot, therefore, be prevented from inventing and using different terminologies. Instead, what can be done is to:

- identify relevant definitions of scientific terms;
- demand that others state to what concepts these terms refer;
- attempt to convince others to drop inadequate formulations;
- suggest standard terminology.

Everyday versus scientific interpretation

The everyday meaning of 'prevention' refers exclusively to actions taken to prevent something before it occurs.

Scientists, however, usually understand the term 'prevention' in a much broader sense, encompassing 'primary', 'secondary' and 'tertiary prevention', as initially defined by Caplan (1964). The COST A-6 WG II suggested splitting 'tertiary prevention' into type A and type B, thus creating four forms of prevention:

- primary prevention to prevent problem onset;
- secondary prevention to intervene if a problem is likely to occur (prevention in high-risk groups) and/or if the problem has not yet fully manifested (prevention of problem manifestation);
- type-A tertiary prevention to deal with fully manifested problems (prevention of further harm among addicts);
- type-B tertiary prevention, or quaternary prevention, to prevent problems from recurring once they have been successfully treated (relapse prevention).

'Evaluation' in everyday parlance is the process of determining whether a technique or strategy is of any value. Central questions include 'does it work?' and 'is it ethically justifiable?' Less important are questions such as 'how does it work?' or 'why does it work?'

The scientific definition of evaluation is quite different, and encompasses a heterogeneous class of concepts ranging from documentation and description via hypotheses that generate exploratory research to hypotheses that test confirmatory research.

If 'prevention' and 'evaluation' are understood according to their everyday meaning, many promising approaches for reducing social and individual problems are not in fact 'prevention' at all, and evaluation would not be feasible because of economic and/or epistemological restraints. If both terms are understood in their scientific sense, however, a wide range of possible interventions can be included and practically all projects can somehow be evaluated. What is offered may be very different from what the customers expect, but according to established scientific standards it is difficult to argue that what is produced is neither prevention nor evaluation.

Some common scientific classification systems for 'evaluation', as well as some newer concepts developed by the COST A-6 WG II, are described below.

Process, outcome, impact (POI) classification (data dimension)

This popular classification (see Clayton and Cattarello, 1991) is based on the kind of data collected:

- process evaluation systematically assesses the process during the execution of the programme;
- outcome evaluation looks at whether or not the programme objectives were met;
- impact evaluation addresses the question, 'did any effects occur that were not explicitly planned?'

Structural, process, outcome (SPO) classification (data dimension)

This classification by Donabedian (1980), developed in the context of quality assurance, is also based on the type of data collected:

- structural data describe the structural conditions of the programme, such as the place of intervention, the qualifications of the programme team and the characteristics of the target group;
- process data describe the parameters of the programme's implementation;
- outcome data describe the effects of the intervention.

Context evaluation (data dimension)

Drug-prevention programmes are developed for certain target groups under specific historic and cultural conditions (the context). Context variables — such as attitudes, knowledge, experiences and fashions — vary from culture to culture and are subject to rapid change. Programmes that are effective under certain contextual conditions may be ineffective or even counterproductive under other conditions, and only by monitoring the context closely can such differences and changes be identified and the necessary adaptations made.

Formative, summative (FS) classification (state-of-the-programme dimension)

This classification by Scriven (1967) refers to the developmental state of the programme being evaluated:

- formative evaluation takes place in the formative phase, while a programme is still being developed;
- summative evaluation takes place in the summative phase, after a programme has been finalised.

Four-phase model of programme development

The COST A-6 WG II suggested extending Scriven's FS classification to a four-phase model of programme development.

- In Phase 1, the 'concept' or 'pre-formative' phase, the prevention concept itself is developed. This purely reflective phase precedes the 'formative phase', starting with the intention to develop a new programme and ending with the first preliminary draft.
- In Phase 2, the 'development' or 'formative' phase, the programme is created based on observation and small-scale trials until a final version with no obvious shortcomings evolves.
- Phase 3, the 'testing' or 'first summative' phase, aims to confirm the effectiveness of the final version, and ideally involves experimental or quasi-experimental designs. If such a global assessment of effectiveness is not feasible, it is usually at least possible to test parts of the causal model behind the prevention approach (partial proof of effectiveness) or to derive effectiveness based on existing empirical evidence (historic deduction of effectiveness).
- In Phase 4, the 'routine' or 'second summative' phase, the tested final version is routinely applied. In this final phase — since effectiveness has already been established — the main emphasis is on quality assurance.

Descriptive, exploratory, confirmatory (DEC) classification (methodological dimension)

A third way to classify evaluation research is as descriptive versus exploratory versus confirmatory evaluation, a concept related to the kinds of conclusions researchers may legitimately draw on epistemological grounds (the methodological dimension).

- Descriptive evaluation is a synonym for collecting and recording data, documenting and categorising phenomena and summarising the findings without directly attempting to formulate new hypotheses and theories.
- Exploratory evaluation goes beyond mere description. Exploratory research ranges from collecting basic information in rather unexplored scientific areas to the hypothesis-driven development of new models and theories. There are no strict rules concerning procedures in exploratory studies. Basically anything with a chance of providing a greater insight into relevant phenomena is possible and legitimate, as long as it is made explicitly clear that the results of the exploratory phase are not final in any sense.
- Confirmatory evaluation is not concerned with discovering new phenomena and/or formulating new hypotheses, but with proving existing ones. Confirmatory evaluation uses the principles of probability theory and inductive statistics to discriminate substantial effects from irrelevant chance effects. If feasible on epistemological and economic grounds, exploratory results should eventually be tested in confirmatory studies.

Internal, external (IE) classification (evaluator dimension)

In the course of programme development and application, who organises and directs the evaluation naturally makes a great deal of difference. These tasks can be carried out by programme developers and/or programme staff (internal evaluation), or by external experts (external evaluation).

Data, state-of-programme, methodological, evaluator (DSME) classification

The COST A-6 WG II suggested integrating all the classification concepts mentioned above into a comprehensive, four-dimensional classification, encompassing:

- data dimension:
  - structural data;
  - process data;
  - outcome data (explicitly expected effects);
  - impact data (effects not explicitly expected);
  - context data;
- state-of-programme dimension:
  - concept phase (pre-formative phase);
  - development phase (formative phase);
  - testing phase (first summative phase);
  - routine phase (second summative phase);
- methodological dimension:
  - descriptive approach;
  - exploratory approach;
  - confirmatory approach;
- evaluator dimension:
  - internal evaluation;
  - external evaluation.

The DSME classification is quite useful for describing evaluation but, despite integrating most scientifically established concepts to classify evaluation, it is by no means complete or sufficient.

Several important forms of evaluation — from needs assessment to efficiency evaluation — are defined below to complete the picture.

Needs assessment

Central to developing or implementing specific drug-prevention programmes is assessing whether or not action is required in a specific problem area, and whether needs are already being adequately met by existing programmes and/or services.

Ethical evaluation

The personal convictions of the evaluators naturally also have a strong impact on any evaluation. Evaluators usually judge immediately whether the techniques and strategies suggested by programme developers and/or used by the programme staff correspond to their personal values and are ethically acceptable to them. Ethical evaluation should therefore be made an explicit topic.

Historical evaluation

A common form of evaluation is expertise based on personal experience and research knowledge. Since this process makes use of existing (historical) data, the label 'historical evaluation' is appropriate.

Methodological evaluation

Methodological evaluation is concerned with whether empirical research is based on an appropriate epistemological and statistical basis.

Feasibility evaluation

If a programme is probably not feasible under real-life conditions, it makes little sense to spend time and effort demonstrating its effectiveness. It is possible to identify lack of feasibility without elaborate and expensive research designs in the formative phase of programme development.

Monitoring unexpected adverse side effects

Monitoring unexpected adverse side effects is a central aspect in every phase of evaluation. The number of potential problem areas is almost unlimited and new undesirable outcomes may arise if the contextual conditions change.

Effectiveness evaluation

Effectiveness evaluation aims to prove that pre-defined goals (specific changes in primary-efficacy variables) can be achieved. If economic or methodological limitations render it impossible to design methodologically adequate experimental or quasi-experimental studies to provide global proof of effectiveness, it is usually at least possible to test parts of the causal model behind the prevention approach (partial proof of effectiveness). In some cases, effectiveness can legitimately be derived from empirically based theory (historical deduction of effectiveness or historical evaluation). If there is strong evidence that a certain strategy works, it does not have to be tested repeatedly.

Quality assurance

The COST A-6 WG II recommended defining quality assurance (QA) as 'evaluation of the quality of implementation under routine conditions', that is, after a programme has been implemented. The idea is to ensure that the level of programme execution does not decline. QA can be organised internally by the programme staff (quality management or QM) and externally by independent evaluators (quality control or QC).

Efficiency evaluation

Efficiency evaluation, not to be confused with effectiveness evaluation, includes cost-effectiveness analyses (CEA) and cost–benefit analyses (CBA). CEA compares the efficiency of approaches aimed at identical goals, while CBA compares the value of the benefits obtained from a programme with the costs of implementing it.

Methodological aspects of evaluating drug prevention

Some of the methodological problems encountered in evaluating primary drug prevention can be easily resolved with appropriate strategies and moderate efforts. Other problems require greater efforts — possibly not justified in many specific situations — and still others create insurmountable economic and/or epistemological research limitations. A few particular methodological problems are addressed below.

Exploratory research presented as confirmatory

The difference between exploratory and confirmatory research is of fundamental importance in science. Both forms of research depend heavily on each other and it is unjustified to consider either approach as having a higher status. Unfortunately, Popper (1934), while stressing the importance of exploratory research, reserved the attribute 'scientific' for confirmatory research. This caused the fateful perception that exploratory research is inferior to confirmatory research and tempted many scientists to present exploratory work as confirmatory. Since journals usually restrict the size of the research articles they carry and often do not really care about the epistemological foundations of research, it is not always easy to identify such fundamental shortcomings in scientific articles.

Many variables treated as primary-efficacy variables

The dichotomy between primary-efficacy and secondary variables is central to specifying outcome variables within confirmatory research projects. Under ideal conditions, confirmatory research projects should have only one primary-efficacy variable. This can be a specific factor or an index generalising over a set of several variables. If one primary-efficacy variable is not feasible, the nominal significance level has to be adjusted to the number of primary-efficacy variables or alpha inflation will jeopardise all significant considerations. This phenomenon is well known to scientists, but very few care about its practical implications.

Inadequate surrogate variables

The dichotomy between efficacy and surrogate variables is based on the concept of indirect measurement via causally linked dimensions — a common procedure in science. Surrogate variables are used to assess phenomena in cases where it is difficult or impossible to assess efficacy variables directly. Popular synonyms for surrogate variables are 'intermediate variables', 'indicator variables' or 'proxy measures'. The use of surrogate variables is justified, given that causal relationships between intermediate variables and efficacy variables have been established through experimental or quasi-experimental research. It is highly questionable, however, whether the causality assumption is based on correlation only. While causality implies correlation, the converse is not the case. In practical research, any correlations in line with research expectations are commonly interpreted causally while implausible correlations are not.

Short-, medium- and long-term effects

In designing prevention programmes, it is the lasting (long-term) effects that are of primary interest, while short- and medium-term effects may play a role as secondary variables to explain the mechanisms leading from specific actions to the desired outcomes. They may also serve as surrogate variables to assess the ultimate problem dimension indirectly, but they are definitely not substitutes for essential long-term effects. Evaluators unable to demonstrate lasting results commonly imply that short-term outcomes are relevant per se, but this reasoning is not really convincing.

Knowledge, attitudes, personality and life skills as outcome variables

Variables such as knowledge, attitudes, personality and life skills commonly play a prominent role in evaluating primary-prevention outcomes and many researchers treat these factors as primary variables to assess effectiveness. Much empirical research suggests that changes in most of these indicators do not result in relevant behavioural change or a reduction in the problem.

Non-linear relationships

The assumption that an average reduction in problem indicators reduces the overall risk of problematic developments in a cohort is widespread but incorrect. Instead, the relationship between indicators and associated problems is commonly 'u-shaped' rather than linear.

According to the 'self-protection/self-medication hypothesis' (Uhl and Springer, 1996), people with severe psychological, psychical and/or social problems tend either to avoid alcohol totally (abstainers) or to consume excessive quantities (problem drinkers). If the average problem level could be successfully reduced through primary prevention, both the number of abstainers and the number of problem drinkers would be expected to fall, resulting in more people consuming alcohol as well as fewer people with alcohol problems. A similar relationship has been demonstrated concerning cannabis.

Protective and risk factors

It is common practice in prevention research to look for variables that correlate with favourable and unfavourable outcomes and to call them 'protective' and 'risk' factors. Some of these elements are 'context variables' that cannot be changed — such as gender or ethnic background — while others are 'intermediate variables' — such as attitudes, level of education or skills — that can be influenced to a varying degree through appropriate interventions.

'Protective' and 'risk' factors function in three ways:

- as 'indicators' to identify high- and low-risk groups, for example to identify target groups for specific secondary preventive measures;
- as 'surrogate variables' to assess indirectly primary-efficacy variables that are hard or impossible to assess directly;
- as 'starting points' for preventive intervention strategies.

The first of these three, the indicator function, is relatively unproblematic, but the surrogate variable and starting-point functions assume causality — a highly problematic assumption if based on correlation studies only.

The problem of heterogeneity

A central, implicit assumption behind many statistical procedures is homogeneity of effects, in other words, the assumption that all subjects react more or less homogeneously to interventions under scrutiny. Whenever the homogeneity assumption is grossly violated, statistical analysis based on this supposition may yield highly misleading results. An illustrative example is the famous Grand Rapid Study (Borkenstein et al., 1964), a milestone in traffic research that related the effects of alcohol consumption to road safety. The data initially seemed to prove that moderate alcohol levels help to reduce traffic accidents. Hurst (1973) re-analysed the data, controlling for heterogeneity (the different drinking patterns of drivers), and showed that the published effect was artificial, caused by the fact that abstainers — who are, of course, always sober — on average cause four times as many accidents as sober drinkers. In all homogeneous cohorts, the accident risk increased monotonously with higher alcohol levels.

Variation over time and context

In empirical research, stable causal relationships over time independent of situational factors (context) are ideal. In drug prevention, this is hardly ever the case. Specific circumstances and susceptibility to certain preventive approaches vary greatly from culture to culture, from subculture to subculture and from cohort to cohort — and all these factors are subject to rapidly changing fashions and trends.

Generativity

'Generativity' describes the common occurrence of small interventions generating unpredictable effects which evoke further unpredictable effects until an abundance of unpredictable and non-reproducible consequences have arisen. According to chaos theory (Steward, 1989), this is a common phenomenon in nature. In some situations, the magnitude of generativity may far outweigh systematic prevention effects. Generativity should not be confused with unanticipated systematic effects that may be included as expected effects in future evaluation.

Power considerations

Programme effects can usually only be realistically proven if:

- problem incidence is high;
- the effects are massive; and/or
- the sample sizes are large.

If a certain issue in a given population, such as the manifestation of problem drug consumption in the total population, has an incidence of less then 0.1 % per year, and if a programme reduces this manifestation by 20 % (relative effect), problem incidence can be expected to fall from 0.1 % to 0.08 % within this year. This is equivalent to an absolute effect of 0.02 % or 1 out of 5 000 people. To have an acceptable chance of proving the intervention outcome requires a total study sample of more than 360 000. Power considerations are commonly neglected in programme evaluation and designs with inadequate-sized samples (under-powered designs) are widespread.

Under-powered designs increase the likelihood of strong publication bias, caused by the fact that such studies that do not yield statistically significant results are hardly ever considered for publication, while under-powered studies containing statistically significant results are readily accepted.

Measurement problems with self-reported consumption

A widespread assessment strategy in drug-prevention evaluation is to use self-reports, a relatively unreliable source of information. The possible magnitude of the bias can be illustrated by a finding from Uhl and Springer (1996) who were confronted with the fact that almost two-thirds of several age cohorts who had already admitted illicit drug use decided not to 'remember' previous drug use 10 years later.

Dependence of observational units

It is common in drug prevention for the observational units to be sampled in clusters or groups (such as school classes) and treated as independent units, causing an increased rate of significance by mere chance. In practical research, this problem is usually solved by simply ignoring it.

Conclusions

Drug prevention and evaluating drug prevention are almost uniformly considered high public priorities. It is self-evident that actions implemented to prevent problems before they occur are superior to interventions established once problems have emerged. Besides, there is a broad consensus that whether or not these interventions produce the desired results should be assessed to optimise strategies. Actions proposed in this context should be well described, feasible, ethically justifiable, effective and cost-efficient, and all this is somehow related to the term 'evaluation'.

Looking critically at the present state of drug prevention and evaluation, there are many fundamental problems. The central terminology is extremely heterogeneous and vague and many people are not aware of this. Sound scientific evidence concerning which concepts are worth pursuing and which are obsolete is scarce, and drug-prevention programmes tend to be either inadequately evaluated or not evaluated at all. In addition, many promising research questions in this field cannot be tackled because of fundamental economic, technical and epistemological limitations.

In spite of all this, researchers, drug-prevention specialists and evaluators have the means to improve drug prevention and evaluation if they have sufficient funds with which to do so and if the public does not expect miracles. Real progress is possible if those in the field are more precise in both terminology and conceptions, are ready to accept basic methodological limitations rather than ignore them and are prepared to admit inevitable uncertainties and accept that some things just cannot be achieved at present. Public pressure to accomplish impossible tasks must be withstood and colleagues who nourish unrealistic expectations because of calculated insincerity or ignorance criticised.

What is therefore needed is concerted action to improve the quality of both drug prevention and evaluation. Important milestones in this endeavour in Europe include the *Handbook prevention* (Van der Stel, 1998), the work of COST A-6 resulting in the publication of Springer and Uhl (1998), the European Monitoring Centre for Drugs and Drug Addiction's *Guidelines for the evaluation of drug prevention* (EMCDDA, 1998) and the implementation of the EMCDDA's Exchange on drug demand-reduction action (EDDRA) information system ([59]).

References

Bloch, A. (1985), *Murphy's law complete*, London, Methuen.

Borkenstein, R. F., Crowther, R. F., Shumate, R. P., Ziel, W. P., Zylman, R. (1964), *The role of the drinking driver in traffic accidents*, Bloomington, IN, Indiana Department of Police Administration, Indiana University.

Caplan, G. (1964), *Principles of preventive psychiatry*, New York, Basic Books.

Clayton, R. R., Cattarello, A. (1991), 'Prevention intervention research: challenges and opportunities', in Leukefeld, C. G., Bukovsky, W. J. (Eds), *Drug abuse prevention intervention research: methodological issues*, Research Monograph 107, Rockville, MD, National Institute on Drug Abuse.

Dalkey, N., Helmer, O. (1963), 'An experimental application of the Delphi Method to the use of experts', *Management Science*, No 3, p. 458.

Donabedian, A. (1980), *Explorations in quality assessment and monitoring. Volume 1. The definition of quality and approaches to its assessment*, Ann Arbor, MI, Health Administration Press.

European Monitoring Centre for Drugs and Drug Addiction (1998), *Guidelines for the evaluation of drug prevention*, Manuals No 1, Lisbon, EMCDDA.

Hurst, P. M. (1973), 'Epidemiological aspects of alcohol in driver crashes and citations', *Journal of Safety Research*, No 5, pp. 130–47.

Lindstone, H. A., Turroff, M. (1975), *The Delphi method: techniques and applications*, Massachusetts, MA, Addison-Wesley.

Popper, K. R. (1934), *The logic of scientific discovery*, eighth revised edition 1975, London, Hutchinson.

Scriven, M. (1967), 'The methodology of evaluation', in Tyler, R. W., Gagne, R. M., Scriven, M. (Eds), *Perspectives of curriculum evaluation*, Chicago, IL, Rand-McNally.

Springer, A., Uhl, A. (Eds) (1998), *Evaluation research in regard to primary prevention of drug abuse*, Brussels: European Commission.

Steward, I. (1989), *Does God play dice? The mathematics of chaos*, London, Penguin.

Uhl, A. (1998), 'Evaluation of primary prevention in the field of illicit drugs: definitions — concepts — problems', in Springer, A., Uhl, A. (Eds), *Evaluation research in regard to primary prevention of drug abuse*, Brussels, European Commission.

([59]) For more on the *Guidelines for the evaluation of drug prevention*, see Chapters 5 and 6. For more on the EDDRA information system, see Chapters 11 and 12.

Uhl, A., Springer, A. (1996), *Studie über den Konsum von Alkohol und psychoaktiven Stoffen in Österreich unter Berücksichtigung problematischer Gebrauchsmuster. Repräsentativerhebung 1993/94*, Vienna, Bundesministerium für Gesundheit und Konsumentenschutz.

Van der Stel, J. (Ed.) (1998), *Handbook prevention: alcohol, drugs and tobacco*, Strasbourg, Pompidou Group of the Council of Europe.

RECOMMENDATIONS AND EVALUATION

PART IV

RECOMMENDATIONS

On the basis of the discussions held during the second European conference on the evaluation of drug prevention, the organisers proposed a number of recommendations that were debated, revised and amended during the conference workshops and approved in the final plenary session. The revised recommendations, which form the final conference conclusions, were presented as one of the last points of the programme. The participants expressed the hope that agreeing on these issues would place the evaluation of drug" prevention higher on the political agenda in Europe.

Evaluation is recognised as a tool for more cost-effective drug-prevention strategies

- Needs assessment and evaluation are essential for effective drug prevention and are an integral part of such programmes and activities at all levels, whether international, national, regional or local.
- Appropriate means (including financial resources) should be available for developing and implementing adequate evaluation protocols for all drug-prevention programmes and projects.
- The need for commonly agreed evaluation quality criteria — such as clear and coherent objectives, goals, purposes and resources available for the programme — is recognised. The EMCDDA's *Guidelines for the evaluation of drug prevention* and its Evaluation instruments bank should be taken into account in developing such criteria [60].
- Close cooperation should be established between the authorities (political and others) and professional bodies dealing with drug prevention in developing any evaluation procedure.
- The evaluation procedure should be devised in close cooperation with the programme designers and implementers as well as with the main players who will use the evaluation results.
- Key programme personnel should be involved in planning the evaluation and all stakeholders should receive continuous feedback during the process.
- Evaluation results should be used for developing new and refining existing drug-prevention programmes and, where appropriate, for selecting which projects should be implemented in practice.
- Evaluation processes, while entailing a financial cost, should ensure that drug-prevention programmes and projects are better focused and more efficient.
- Proper needs assessment must be included at the initial stage of any evaluation and should serve as an instrument for feedback during the evaluation process.

---

(60) For more on the *Guidelines for the evaluation of drug prevention*, see Chapters 5 and 6. For more on the Evaluation instruments bank, see Chapter 6.

- Target groups should be considered the key source of information in the needs assessment. Taking account of the ethnographic factors in the target groups' social context (norms, values, lifestyles) is more likely to enhance their acceptance of an intervention.
- Mapping is a dynamic and proactive aspect of assessing the needs of target groups that requires qualitative and innovative methods in addition to traditional questionnaire surveys.
- Internal evaluation of projects and programmes is essential and should be undertaken throughout the planning and implementation phases.
- The stakeholders and actors involved in a drug-prevention programme should establish whether additional, external evaluation is required before the project or programme is initiated. The external evaluator's involvement should last at least for the duration of the project or programme.
- Continuous feedback between programme implementers and evaluators should be ensured throughout the process.
- Those involved in developing and planning drug-prevention strategies should receive training in conceptualising, designing and evaluating social interventions to facilitate the integration of evaluation at the planning stage.
- All those involved in planning and implementing drug-prevention projects should receive adequate training in evaluation processes and methodology.
- Evaluation training programmes at all levels should be set up. The EMCDDA could be invited to play an advisory role in this.
- The exchange of knowledge and tools in the field of drug-prevention evaluation should be reinforced at European level.
- Appropriate exchanges of experience in the field of evaluation methodology (including practical examples) with international organisations and selected third countries are to be encouraged.
- Information on evaluation results and research should be compiled at national and European level and published as a resource for programme planners.
- Mechanisms should be developed to facilitate the dialogue between practitioners and policy-makers on what evaluation findings mean for the further development of drug-prevention programmes.
- The added value of international guidelines for evaluating drug prevention is acknowledged. Nevertheless, it is crucial to adapt these to cultural specificities.
- The need for further research into evaluation is recognised and should be encouraged, in particular at EU level.
- Special attention should be focused on the evaluation needs and corresponding training and logistic requirements in the candidate countries for accession to the European Union (61).

At its meeting on 12 to 14 January 2000, the EMCDDA Management Board suggested (as had some participants at the conference) that these 24 recommendations be condensed and given clear headings. Accordingly, and without loss of content, the

(61) The candidate countries for accession to the European Union are Bulgaria, Cyprus, Czech Republic, Estonia, Hungary, Latvia, Lithuania, Malta, Poland, Romania, Slovakia, Slovenia and Turkey.

EMCDDA reduced the 24 recommendations to 15 and introduced the 'labels' given below.

- **Improve prevention:** evaluation processes, while entailing a financial cost, should ensure that drug-prevention programmes and projects are better focused and more efficient.
- **Means for evaluation:** appropriate means (including financial resources) should be available for developing and implementing adequate evaluation protocols for all drug-prevention programmes and projects.
- **Importance of needs assessment:** needs assessment and evaluation are essential for effective drug prevention and are an integral part of programmes and activities at all levels, whether international, national, regional or local. Proper needs assessment must be included at the initial stage of any evaluation and should serve as an instrument for feedback during the evaluation process.
- **Establish quality criteria based on EMCDDA achievements:** the need for commonly agreed evaluation quality criteria — such as clear and coherent objectives, goals, purposes and resources available for the programme — is recognised. The EMCDDA's *Guidelines for the evaluation of drug prevention* and its Evaluation instruments bank should be taken into account in developing such criteria. The added value of international guidelines for evaluating drug prevention is acknowledged. Nevertheless, it is crucial to adapt these to cultural specificities.
- **Cooperative development:** close cooperation should be established between the authorities (political and others) and professional bodies dealing with drug prevention in developing any evaluation procedure.
- **Involve actors and stakeholders in evaluation:** the evaluation procedure should be devised in close cooperation with the programme designers and implementers as well as with the main players who will use the evaluation results. Key programme personnel should be involved in planning the evaluation and all stakeholders should receive continuous feedback during the process.
- **Make effective use of evaluation results:** evaluation results should be used for developing new and refining existing drug-prevention programmes and, where appropriate, for selecting which projects should be implemented in practice.
- **Interpret evaluation results adequately:** mechanisms should be developed to facilitate the dialogue between practitioners and policy-makers on what evaluation findings mean for the further development of drug-prevention programmes.
- **Role of internal evaluation:** internal evaluation of projects and programmes is essential and should be undertaken throughout the planning and implementation phases.
- **Role of external evaluation:** the stakeholders and actors involved in a drug-prevention programme should establish whether additional, external evaluation is required before the project or programme is initiated. The external evaluator's involvement should last at least for the duration of the project or programme.
- **Training in evaluation, for different levels and audiences:** evaluation training programmes at all levels should be set up:
  - for those involved in developing prevention strategies to facilitate the integration of evaluation at the planning stage;
  - for those involved in planning and implementing drug-prevention projects.

  The EMCDDA could play an advisory role in developing such training courses and facilities.

- **Exchange of skills and experiences within the EU and with third countries:** the exchange of knowledge and tools in the field of drug-prevention evaluation should be reinforced at European level as well as with international organisations and third countries, especially with a view to the evaluation needs and corresponding training and logistic requirements in the candidate countries for accession to the European Union. Therefore, information on evaluation results and research should be compiled at national and European level and published as a resource for programme planners. The EMCDDA's Exchange on drug demand-reduction action (EDDRA) information system should be considered an important instrument for such exchange of experiences (62).
- **Use ethnographic research for evaluation:** taking account of the ethnographic factors in the target groups' social context (norms, values, lifestyles) is more likely to enhance their acceptance of an intervention, and target groups should be considered the key source of information in the needs-assessment process.
- **Integrate innovative methods:** needs assessment among target groups and client-based evaluation require innovative and qualitative methods in addition to traditional questionnaire surveys. Mapping is a dynamic and proactive example of such methods.
- **Develop new approaches:** the need for further research into evaluation is recognised and should be encouraged, in particular at EU level.

(62) For more on the EDDRA information system, see Chapters 11 and 12.

Evaluation of the second European conference on the evaluation of drug prevention

Ulrik Solberg

A conference on evaluation would not be credible if it were not itself evaluated. The EMCDDA therefore prepared two questionnaires, one to assess the conference in general, and one to evaluate the workshop sessions. The questionnaires consisted of a series of open and closed questions and were relatively brief. The general evaluation questionnaire was distributed at the start of the final plenary session to be returned at the close of the conference, while participants were requested to complete the workshop questionnaire at the end of each session. A total of 93 general evaluation and 159 workshop questionnaires were completed.

The evaluation of the second European conference on the evaluation of drug prevention was affected to some extent by two unforeseen external events. First, a transport strike on the second day of the meeting caused much disruption and led to serious delays in the agenda. Second, a short-circuit left the final conference session without translation facilities for some time before the participants were moved to another room.

Overall evaluation of the conference

The following overall evaluation of the conference is based on the 93 questionnaires completed. The results of quantitative analysis of the closed questions are set out in Table 1.

Table 1: General evaluation of the conference

Question	Average response [a]
1. How important to you were the following aspects of the second European conference on the evaluation of drug prevention (before participating)?	
Acquaintance with evaluation techniques	2.62
'Brushing-up' your knowledge	2.66
Scientific-level presentations	2.46
Professional exchange with colleagues	1.97
Informal communication with other participants	2.04

Question	Average response ([a])
2. How would you rate coverage of the abovementioned aspects?	
Acquaintance with evaluation techniques	3.76
'Brushing-up' your knowledge	3.38
Scientific-level presentations	3.22
Professional exchange with colleagues	2.41
Informal communication with other participants	2.33
3. What effects will the conference have on future evaluation practice?	
It will change evaluation practice for the better	3.00
It will focus political attention on the issue	2.73
It will improve the quality of future evaluations	2.86
4. What aspects would you find most interesting at a future evaluation conference?	
Acquaintance with evaluation techniques	1.87
'Brushing-up' your knowledge	2.09
Scientific-level presentations	1.79
Professional exchange with colleagues	1.66
Social programme	2.74
5. How would you rate the following organisational aspects of the evaluation conference?	
Overall efficiency of the organisation	2.28
Quality of the meeting rooms	1.83
Technical aspects of the conference	2.50
Length of the conference	2.63
Social programme	2.38
Accommodation	3.06
Meals	2.76

NB:
The number of registered participants was set at 150 as nine people were either organisers or only took part in the conference for a day and therefore did not complete the general evaluation questionnaire. The estimated response rate was 62 %.
([a]) On a scale from 1 (the most positive reply) to 6, the average being 3.5.

Analysis of the general conference-evaluation questionnaires reveals that the two most popular aspects of the conference were 'professional exchange with colleagues' and 'informal communication with other participants'. Conversely, the least interesting aspects for the participants were 'acquaintance with evaluation techniques' and '"brushing-up" your knowledge'.

By comparing replies to question 1 on expectations with those to question 2 on outcome it is clear that none of the expectations were fully met — in other words, expectations were higher than the perceived outcome. However, it should be noted that the two aspects that shared the highest expectations — 'professional exchange with colleagues' and 'informal communication with other participants' — were judged to have been the best covered, receiving ratings of 2.41 and 2.33 respectively. Furthermore, the difference between the figures for expectations and those for outcome is smaller for questions 1 and 2 than for the other questions (around 0.35). One interpretation for this might be that the participants were already very well acquainted with evaluation methodology and therefore found little new in the conference presentations, whereas they found interaction with other participants more rewarding.

Responses to question 3 on the effects of future evaluation practice show modest but confident expectations, with replies all more positive than the average value of 3.5. This again might suggest a very competent audience.

If the replies to questions 1 and 2 are compared to those to question 4, it is noteworthy that despite the high rating of 'informal communication with other participants' in questions 1 and 2, 'social programme' is rated lowest in question 4. This suggests that informal communication with other participants is not perceived only in the framework of official dinners, but much more in terms of informal meetings in the corridors during the conference. Question 4 does, however, confirm that the most important aspect of a conference is considered to be 'professional exchange with colleagues', as this is once again ranked highest.

Question number 5 on satisfaction with the overall organisation of the conference gave quite high ratings. A vote of 2.28 showed that the participants were very satisfied with the overall organisation and particularly with the quality of the meeting rooms which received a vote of 1.83.

The comments made in the open questions included the following:

- 12 participants stated that the workshops were too short and three mentioned the need for more concrete themes for these sessions. The bus strike caused a 'force majeure' that was especially detrimental to the workshops.
- 10 questionnaires complained of a lack of simultaneous interpretation into Spanish during the workshops.
- Six people said they were dissatisfied with the recommendations: two found the process of formulating these points too fast and undemocratic; two found them too general; one was afraid of the implications; and one found the large number of recommendations rendered them meaningless.
- Four entries stated that the conference speakers should have been given more time for their presentations.

Some observations diverged. For example, two participants thought that the level of the conference was too high, while another two thought that it was too low. Similarly, some thought that there should have been a greater focus on methodology and research while others had expected a more practical approach.

Of the positive comments, eight participants stated that the conference had been well organised and congratulated the EMCDDA staff responsible for it.

Evaluation of the workshops

The conference participants were expected to register for one of three workshops in each of two workshop blocks. The themes of the workshops were:

- First block:
  - needs assessment;
  - the costs and benefits of evaluation;
  - common goals for policy-makers and professionals.
- Second block:
  - evaluation skills;
  - improving prevention quality criteria through evaluation;
  - transferring experience.

The results of evaluating the completed evaluation questionnaires are set out in Table 2.

Table 2: Evaluation of the workshops

	Workshop 1	Workshop 2	Workshop 3	Workshop 4	Workshop 5	Workshop 6
Questionnaires received	n = 49	n = 10	n = 32	n = 23	n = 31	n = 14
Registered participants	n = 50	n = 19	n = 40	n = 25	n = 52	n = 20
Estimated response rate ([a])	98 %	53 %	80 %	92 %	60 %	70 %
Question	**Average response ([b])**					
	Workshop 1	**Workshop 2**	**Workshop 3**	**Workshop 4**	**Workshop 5**	**Workshop 6**
1. How would you rate the following aspects of the workshops?						
Scientific level	3.31	3.80	3.03	2.22	3.21	2.71
Practical relevance for your work	3.06	3.70	3.00	2.65	3.30	2.21
Exchange of new information	3.10	3.90	2.93	2.70	3.17	2.36
2. How would you rate the following issues?						
Personal interest in the subject	1.94	2.10	1.77	1.73	2.03	1.57
Quality of participants	2.56	3.10	2.16	1.82	2.38	1.64
Overall satisfaction with session	3.15	3.60	2.70	2.15	2.90	2.14
3. How would you rate the extent to which the topics discussed corresponded to what had been announced beforehand?	2.76	3.40	2.24	1.95	2.73	2.00

NB:

([a]) This figure is based on the number of completed questionnaires divided by the number of registered participants in each workshop.

([b]) On a scale from 1 (the most positive reply) to 6, with the average being 3.5.

It should be noted that the numbers registered for each block of workshops do not correspond to the 160 who participated in the conference as a whole since this figure includes the organisers, speakers who only attended the conference for one day and participants who did not register in advance.

Evaluation of the workshop questionnaires reveals that workshop 4 on evaluation skills and workshop 6 on transferring experience were the most popular. These sessions both score highly on the participants' overall satisfaction, interest in the subject and the quality of the participants.

All participants reported very high personal interest in the subject of the workshops of their choice with these ratings ranging from 1.57 to 2.10, whereas relevance to practical work was somewhat lower with ratings from 2.21 to 3.70. 'Scientific level' and 'exchange of new information' came lower still with averages from 2.22 to 3.80 and from 2.36 to 3.90 respectively.

In general, however, the conference participants appear to have been satisfied overall with the workshop sessions as only one received ratings on the negative side of the average value of 3.5.

General conclusions

GENERAL CONCLUSIONS

Margareta Nilson

What is evaluation?

I breath, therefore I evaluate', Jacques A. Bury said in the opening speech of the second European conference on the evaluation of drug prevention. In any activity, the objectives and how best to meet them are defined, results are examined and, if they are not satisfactory, the activity is modified. In the context of health promotion and drug prevention, evaluation is a procedure by which to determine, obtain, analyse and disseminate information to allow decisions to be made based on scientific facts rather than mere speculation.

As Rui Rodrigues stated, it is very encouraging for those committed to evaluation that whether or not to evaluate is no longer at issue, although when and what to evaluate — and why — still need to be determined. Sabine Haas pointed out that despite the growing demand for, and interest in, evaluation in the EU, the necessary skills are still greatly lacking. In central and eastern Europe, confronting the drug phenomenon has become such an urgent need since the early 1990s that despite the recognition that evaluation is important, interventions are often implemented when no evidence exists to justify them or to indicate their effectiveness.

However, to avoid the impossible search for perfection from incapacitating the field altogether, Alfred Uhl recommended that the basic methodological limitations of evaluation be accepted rather than ignored, the inevitable uncertainties surrounding it acknowledged, and the fact that some things simply cannot be accomplished at present recognised.

Involving all parties: a key issue

Those deciding on an evaluation and those implementing the programmes being evaluated must all agree on their objectives, and have the necessary skills and knowledge to fulfil their respective roles. Evaluation can only achieve its aim if all the parties concerned — whether political decision-makers, funding authorities, evaluators, drug-prevention professionals or their target groups — are fully involved. From a bottom-up perspective, the motivation and understanding of all actors is essential. Drug-prevention professionals and their target groups must be convinced of the utility of evaluation and not fear it. From a top-down perspective, the commitment of decision-makers and funding authorities is essential in order to make available the resources required to conduct the evaluation properly and in order to ensure that the results will be taken into consideration.

The quality of an evaluation depends on the reliability of the data collected as well as on the awareness of all those involved of the utility of the exercise. Many of the conference participants had very strong opinions on this issue, and good knowledge and acceptance of the evaluation procedure is clearly a key factor in assuring the validity of the results.

There are arguments both for and against internal and external evaluations, and most of the participants agreed that a combination of internal and external evaluation is the most rewarding approach.

The funds allocated to evaluate a programme clearly affect its implementation. Jacques A. Bury proposed that the evaluation budget should be between 2 and 15 % of the global programme budget, and the more innovative and visible the project, the higher the budget should be. Clearly under no illusions, he stated that the most common way to sabotage an evaluation is to under-finance it.

Promoting evaluation techniques

Needs assessment

Needs assessment is a prerequisite both for implementing a drug-prevention programme and for its evaluation. Prevalence data and analysis on a macro level, such as the European school survey project on alcohol and other drugs (ESPAD) study, can be useful, but more local investigations, for example into new patterns of drug use, or those focusing on a restricted population like a particular school or neighbourhood, are usually necessary for 'fine-tuning'. In his presentation, Mark Morgan demonstrated that the specific cultural needs of different target groups can have a major impact on what does and does not work.

Process evaluation

Process evaluation uses a systematic approach to assess how a programme works in its environment. The quality of the programme delivery might, for example, have an important effect on its routine implementation. Process evaluation also examines unexpected effects. An example of process evaluation was given by Krzysztof Ostaszewski's description of the Program Domowych Detektywów which illustrated the role of qualitative evaluation methods in the cross-cultural adaptation of a drug-prevention programme and the assessment of its effectiveness, as well as the way it was modified according to the evaluation results.

Outcome evaluation

Outcome evaluation measures whether the objectives of a specific programme have been fulfilled. This enables programme-makers to provide evidence of the outputs of their work — in other words, what has been achieved by the money they have spent, the posts they have created and the time they have allocated. However, outcome-evaluation data can only be interpreted with background knowledge of the progress and should never stand alone. Such data can even be useful for identifying flaws in programme delivery, as occurred in Program Domowych Detektywów.

Clear indicators and targets for outcomes are crucial, but, as Mark Morgan pointed out, they can be misleading if intermediate variables are relied upon. Amador Calafat questioned the use of 'classical' intermediate variables, such as self-esteem and social skills, and highlighted the need for awareness of the specific objective of the drug-prevention programme: does the expected outcome actually reduce drug problems?

Convincing policy-makers

Susanne Schardt from the European Cities on Drug Policy network pointed out that in order to give policy-makers the concrete support and synthetic advice they need for informed decision-making, scientific evaluation results need to be 'translated' into an appropriate form. It is not enough to present this information clearly; it must also be transposed into clear policy options in an effort to bridge the gap between science and policy.

Policy-makers love statistics, Schardt stated, and use them to assess what measures are being implemented in other settings and to compare the effectiveness of those strategies with their own. In this way, politicians can be convinced to use evaluation results either to communicate what they think should be done, to reject what they do not want to do, or to legitimise what they will do anyway.

Tom Bucke gave some interesting examples of how to have an impact on policy-makers.

- The effect of evaluation on policy depends above all on timing and recognising opportunities. Providing policy-makers with evidence of effectiveness when they need it can have a major impact on practice, but results that appear too late are useless.
- Evaluations do not have to be large and resource-intensive to influence practice. Applying examples of effective drug-prevention practice from the international literature to a specific country — with due adaptation to the respective cultural context — is one way of seeking to shape practice. The media can be an important partner in publicising evaluation results and bringing public opinion to bear on policy.
- Negative evaluation findings can be just as valuable as positive ones. Evaluation may highlight approaches which were not very effective, but instead of being interpreted as 'prevention does not work', such results should lead practitioners to develop more effective approaches and more efficient practice.

Using the example of the Galician plan on drugs, Manuel Araujo Gallego showed that, with the good will of policy-makers, a whole regional demand-reduction strategy can be systematically evaluated.

From theory to practice

The workshop sessions developed specific practical themes in a more informal setting. The following are some of the most inspiring points raised during these sessions.

- The main benefit of evaluation lies in the systematic learning process through success and failure.
- Evaluation should be included in all drug-prevention interventions, regardless of the size of their budget.
- Drug prevention should not, however, be too restricted by evaluation requirements as this could inhibit new initiatives.
- Process evaluation should not be neglected. This may require more investment in identifying adequate methodologies.
- International and national seminars should be organised to spread evaluation knowledge and skills.
- Quality is not only a scientific concept, but is also relevant at both the practical and political level. The quality of an evaluation can be enhanced by defining objectives and methods which then determine the appropriate choice of evaluation indicators.
- While quality standards are essential, they can be difficult to define, although there is consensus about minimal quality criteria. Guiding principles might be:
  - consistence and coherence;
  - operational indicators;
  - consensus among, and participation of, all actors;
  - the equal importance of process and outcome evaluation.
- There are both similarities and differences in the goals of policy-makers and drug-prevention professionals, as well as in the nature of the dialogue between them and the role that evaluation can play to facilitate this dialogue.
- Dialogue and communication skills are essential to create understanding among professionals and policy-makers of their respective goals and needs. To this end, several countries have established either formal structures at national or local level or other mechanisms to facilitate this communication. These structures must now establish their legitimacy by providing better-quality drug prevention.
- Information must be increasingly well structured to enable all parties to find their way through the 'information jungle'.
- There should be a balance between old and new technologies, and it should be borne in mind that many grass-roots workers do not have access to the Internet.
- Electronic communication and the Internet, however essential they are for information exchange, cannot substitute human networking. Training, networking, individual contacts and personal feedback thus remain vital.

The Reitox national focal points have a crucial role to play in promoting the evaluation of drug prevention. In this context, it will be necessary to increase their visibility and ensure they receive the recognition and support they need at both national and European level.

The EMCDDA's support for drug-prevention professionals

Annual report on the state of the drugs problem in the European Union

The EMCDDA's annual report provides a valuable overview of the drug situation in Europe and of what is being done to change it ([63]). Although including more information about activities at local level has been requested, the report relies on the information the EMCDDA receives from its national focal points which may not always have access to the national networks necessary to obtain this information.

Guidelines for the evaluation of drug prevention

Christoph Kröger's model of eight stages of readiness includes the phases of initiation, standardisation and professionalisation. While the evaluation of drug prevention has clearly passed the initiation stage, it has not yet reached the standardisation phase and this should now be the aim of all drug-prevention practitioners. It will, however, take much longer to reach the professional stage.

The EMCDDA *Guidelines for the evaluation of drug prevention* are valuable in this context, and their implementation and adaptation at national level are encouraging ([64]). It has become clear that the more institutionalised the distribution of the guidelines in a particular country, the more members of the target group receive them.

Exchange on drug demand-reduction action

The Exchange on drug demand-reduction action (EDDRA) information system was created to promote the development of an evaluation culture ([65]). Few demand-reduction projects in Europe are being, or have been, evaluated, and collecting and disseminating information that does not exist is clearly an impossible challenge. But far from being seen as an obstacle, this fundamental limitation is itself a strength and should allow the development of a European-wide evaluation culture to be both monitored and quantified. As a largely unintended by-product, EDDRA has also proved to be a useful training and communication instrument.

Evaluation instruments bank

The Evaluation instruments bank (EIB) includes quality evaluation tools devised for specific situations and/or target groups, guidelines for their use and related literature ([66]). The EMCDDA will establish a mailing list from the entries in the EIB database to ensure continuing dialogue and feedback.

([63]) *Annual report on the state of the drugs problem in the European Union*, Lisbon, EMCDDA, 1995, 1997, 1998, 1999.

([64]) *Guidelines for the evaluation of drug prevention*, Manuals No 1, Lisbon, EMCDDA, 1998.

([65]) The EDDRA system is available at (http://www.emcdda.org/databases/databases_eddra.shtml).

([66]) The Evaluation instruments bank will be available via the EMCDDA website in 2000.

Training in evaluation practice and the EDDRA system

Training seminars in evaluation practice and how to use the EDDRA system, attended by the national focal points and other national experts, have proved very useful and will be continued. Through these seminars, the EMCDDA can motivate national evaluators and enhance their skills.

Other issues: treatment, outreach work, criminal-justice system

The EMCDDA's work on evaluation does not stop with drug prevention. Together with the World Health Organisation, the Centre began disseminating workbooks for the evaluation of treatment from 2000 onwards. It is also launching a project to develop evaluation guidelines for outreach work and for demand-reduction activities in the criminal-justice system. Gradually, it is hoped to build up a pool of expertise in the area of evaluation which will come close to the help desk that Sabine Haas proposed.

Future perspectives

The EMCDDA is increasing its information-collection and dissemination role at EU level. In so doing, it is taking advantage of the opportunities offered by Community programmes, above all the European Union Drugs Strategy (2000–04). In addition, the Community action programme for the prevention of drug dependence has been extended to the end of 2002, and there may be further benefits from the fifth framework programme, which includes a drug and drug-addiction component [67].

All this underlines that the results of the second European conference on the evaluation of drug prevention are wider than simply the recommendations it adopted, and this richness will be integrated into the routine work of the EMCDDA. As both Françoise Moyen and Saini Mustalampi pointed out, evaluation will be an integral part of all Community initiatives and programmes in the framework of the new EU drugs strategy — an aspect that will be stressed by the French Presidency of the EU in 2000 — and the EMCDDA will contribute to this integration. The EMCDDA will also provide the European Commission with the recommendations and conclusions of the second European conference on the evaluation of drug prevention to facilitate appropriate follow-up at Community level.

(67) Information on the Community action programme for the prevention of drug dependence is available at (http://europa.eu.int/comm/health/ph/programmes/drugs/index_en.htm). The fifth framework programme defines the European Union's strategic priorities for research and technological development for the period 1998 to 2002. For further details, see (http://www.cordis.lu/fp5/home.html).

CONTRIBUTORS

CONTRIBUTORS

Pavel Bem
National Drug Commission of the Czech Republic
Nabrezi Edwarda Benese 4
Prague 1, Mala Strana
11801 Czech Republic
Tel. (420-2) 20 18 91 51
Fax (420-2) 31 14 4

Alexandre Berlin
Rue Philippe le Bon 24
B-1000 Brussels
Tel. (32-2) 231 01 52

Tom Bucke
Drug Prevention Advisory Service Room 314
Horseferry House
Dean Ryle Street
London SW1P 2AW
United Kingdom
Tel. (44-20) 7217 8492/31
Fax (44-20) 7217 8230

Jacques A. Bury
Institute of Social and Preventive Medicine
Medical University Centre
CH-1211 Geneva
Switzerland
Tel. (41-22) 702 59 19
Fax (41-22) 702 59 12

Amador Calafat
Institut de Recherches Européen sur les Facteurs de Risque chez l'Enfant et l'Adolescent (Irefrea)
Rambla, No 15-2º, 3ª
E-07003 Palma de Mallorca
Tel. (34) 971 72 74 34
Fax (34) 971 21 33 06

Manuel Araujo Gallego
Plan de Galicia sobre drogas
Edificio Administrativo San Caetano, 2-2°
E-15771 Santiago de Compostela
Tel. (34) 981 54 18 59/60/66
Fax (34) 981 54 18 65

Sabine Haas
Österreichisches Bundesinstitut für Gesundheitswesen (ÖBIG)
Stubenring 6
A-1010 Vienna
Tel. (43-1) 515 61-160
Fax (43-1) 513 84 72

Joana Judice
European Forum for Urban Security
38, rue Liancourt
F-75014 Paris
Tel. (33) 140 64 49 00/13
Fax (33) 140 64 49 10

Christoph Kröger
Institut für Therapieforschung (IFT)
Parzivalstraße 25
D-80804 Munich
Tel. (49-89) 36 08 04 60
Fax (49-89) 36 08 04 59

Mark Morgan
St Patrick's College
Drumcondra
Dublin 9
Ireland
Tel. (353-1) 837 61 91
Fax (353-1) 837 61 97

Krzysztof Ostaszewski
Institute of Psychiatry and Neurology
Department of Mental Health Promotion
Youth Prevention Unit
Sobieskiego Str. 1/9
02-957 Warsaw
Poland
Tel. (48-22) 642 66 11 ext. 330
Fax (48-22) 642 53 75

Teresa Salvador-Llivina
Centro de Estudios sobre la Promoción de la Salud (CEPS)
C/ Carretera de Humera, 60
E-28224 Pozuelo de Alarcón, Madrid
Tel. (34) 913 51 53 61
Fax (34) 913 51 53 37

Susanne Schardt
European Cities on Drug Prevention (ECDP)
Niddastraße 64
D-60329 Frankfurt am Main
Tel. (49-69) 233 013
Fax (49-69) 242 48 308

Alfred Uhl
The Ludwig Bolzmann Institute on Addiction Research
Mackgasse 7–9
A-1237 Vienna
Tel. (43-1) 888 41 37 38
Fax (43-1) 888 25 33 77

EMCDDA

George Estievenart
Margareta Nilson
Gregor Burkhart
Philippe Roux
Ulrik Solberg

European Monitoring Centre for Drugs and Drug Addiction (EMCDDA)
Rua da Cruz de Santa Apolónia 23–25
P-1149-045 Lisbon
Tel. (351) 21 811 30 00
Fax (351) 21 813 17 11

Practical Information

Address:

European Monitoring Centre for Drugs and Drug Addiction (EMCDDA)
Rua da Cruz de Santa Apólonia 23–25
P-1149-045 Lisbon

Tel.

(351) 21 811 30 00

Fax

(351) 21 813 17 11

E-mail:

info@emcdda.org

Website:

http://www.emcdda.org

EMCDDA, August 2000

European Monitoring Centre for Drugs and Drug Addiction

EMCDDA Scientific Monograph Series No 5
Evaluation: a key tool for improving drug prevention

Luxembourg: Office for Official Publications of the European Communities

2000 — 184 pp. — 16 x 24 cm

ISBN 92-9168-105-9

Price (excluding VAT) in Luxembourg: EUR 16.50